This is
Rugby

This is Rugby

GEORGE HOOK

HACHETTE
BOOKS
IRELAND

First published in 2013 by Hachette Books Ireland

A CIP catalogue record for this title is available from the British Library.

ISBN 978 1444 743 999

Book text design and typesetting by Anú Design, Tara
Printed and bound by Butler Tanner & Dennis Ltd

Hachette Books Ireland policy is to use papers that are natural, renewable and recyclable products and made from wood grown in sustainable forests. The logging and manufacturing processes are expected to conform to the environmental regulations of the country of origin.

Hachette Books Ireland
8 Castlecourt Centre
Castleknock
Dublin 15, Ireland

A division of Hachette UK Ltd.
338 Euston Road
London NW1 3BH
www.hachette.ie

To my father

CONTENTS

CONTENTS

Foreword

The year was 1998, the late, great Tim O'Connor, the then Head of RTÉ Sport, assigned me, an inexperienced twenty-six-year-old, to be editor of RTÉ rugby programmes. The mission as Tim saw it was to create a brand for RTÉ rugby, adding to the strength of presenter Bill O'Herlihy and our commentary teams of Fred Cogley, Tony Ward, Ralph Keyes and Jim Sherwin – 1999 was a World Cup year, and we needed a new panel to bed down quickly.

The problem as we saw it was a lack of consistency, there was too much variation. So, why not copy what had been done with RTÉ's soccer coverage – changes there had enabled the public to identify instantly with the panel of John Giles, Eamon Dunphy and Bill O'Herlihy. They had become a byword for excellence in sports analysis: occasionally infuriating, always challenging the consensus, invariably an excellent watch.

The other problem with our rugby coverage was that it pandered a little too much to those on the inside, the people who had played rugby and knew all of the nuances of the tactics and rules. As a person who loved rugby, I always felt that the elitism within the sport was one of the biggest obstacles to its growth in Ireland. Most of our audience for the Six Nations hadn't gone to Blackrock College or Pres Cork, yet they were enthusiastic supporters of their country and were increasingly tuning in to watch Munster and Leinster. We needed to make the sport more accessible so that it could include everyone, not just those who grew up playing the game.

The timing could not have been better: this was just two years before Brian O' Driscoll's hat-trick in Paris which shot the starting pistol on a golden era for Irish rugby at both provincial and international level. O'Driscoll, along with Paul O'Connell and Ronan O'Gara, were the poster boys for RTÉ throughout this period and made even more people want to follow the Irish team.

Prior to 1998, George Hook and Brent Pope had been brought in sporadically to be part of our analysis team, but neither had nailed down a first-team spot. As we were in search of a fresh start, I proposed George and Brent as our good cop–bad cop combination. Tim asked me to see if Tom McGurk would take on the task of leading the coverage. Later the former Irish captain and full-back Conor O'Shea joined and became a hugely influential and important part of the team. With the inclusion of Ryle Nugent as a new commentator, the transformation was complete.

And so it began, an occasionally maddening, often hilarious but always exciting time, incorporating coverage of Heineken Cup titles for both Ulster and Munster, an Irish Grand Slam and several Triple Crowns. Managers and players have come and gone, but Hook, Pope, O'Shea and McGurk continue to provoke, illuminate and entertain.

George has a fantastic rugby brain and ability to remember facts and figures which is slightly disconcerting and sometimes borders on the obsessive. Work has never been an issue for him, research and effort were always primary, providing a fantastic example to those who worked with him. He has always created a magnificent team ethos, even if he drove the team mad most of the time!

To those who do not know him, it may be surprising that someone with such a big personality could be such a good team player. For him, the performance of the team was always the priority. Before the 1999 Rugby World Cup in Wales, he suggested that we ask the former Australian coach Alan Jones to join us on the panel. Alan was an experienced orator and radio broadcaster who had excellent rugby credentials. As a newly installed rugby panellist, George might have feared that someone like Jones would overshadow him – but George knew that our coverage would be richer for having Jones on the panel and so the entire team would benefit as a result. It was an inspired choice and Jones gelled with our newly constituted panel and there is no doubt in my mind the public benefited as a result.

Above all, George is a brilliant communicator and storyteller. One thing I always admired about him is that, not unlike O'Driscoll or O'Gara, he was able to spot a gap and exploit it. George truly grabbed hold of the opportunity given to him by RTÉ and the *Sunday Independent* and turned it into a life-changing career move in his fifties; he is an example to us all that it is never too late to change your circumstances, if you are prepared to work hard and believe in your ability.

George is also an inveterate worrier. I recall meeting him in Jury's Ballsbridge at eight o'clock on the morning of a Six Nations game, to discover that he had been in the hotel Coffee Dock since 4 a.m. going over his lines, double-checking facts and rehearsing his analysis pieces.

I am happy to say George has calmed down since then – possibly because he has cut down on the forty cups of coffee a day, or maybe it's because he and Ingrid have found that becoming grandparents suits them. Ultimately, I think George has finally found happiness and contentment in his life; it took him a long time but he discovered something he loves doing, combining as it does his love of rugby and communication.

A book such as this is the perfect territory for someone like George. It challenges the consensus, creates a polemic, involves the construction of arguments for and against and contains a smattering of fiction! In *This is Rugby*, he has RTÉ Sport's Hugh Cahill to contend with, representing the views of a younger breed of rugby enthusiast.

Hook will always divide opinion, this book may infuriate or frustrate you, but you certainly won't find it dull – and, who knows, you may even find yourself agreeing with him.

Glen Killane, Managing Director of Television, RTÉ

'Never be afraid
to have an opinion.
Never be influenced
by others. However
unpopular it may be,
hold your ground.'

My father

Introduction

This book is dedicated to my father because I am certain that without his commitment to parenthood, I would be a very different person today. I also strongly suspect that I share some of his weaknesses, although they were never obvious to me when he was alive.

The past twenty years of my life have made an enormous difference to my financial well-being and the health of my marriage. It seems incredible looking back on my life that I was in my mid-fifties before I discovered my true vocation in life.

I can remember very well the day my father implanted in me the seeds of debate that today form the core of my broadcasting career. We invariably went to 11:15 a.m. mass in St Augustine's church in Cork and afterwards would walk for an hour or so while he regaled me with tales of heroism from the Second World War, the fight for Irish freedom and, above all, stories of every sport.

By the age of twelve, I knew all about the Bodyline series in cricket, the Triple Crowns and Grand Slam of the Irish rugby team and every heavyweight boxing champion since John L. Sullivan. My father did more than give me a love of sport; he gave me the belief to have the courage of your convictions.

I remember one Sunday very clearly. We were strolling up the Western Road in Cork to spend some time in the museum in Fitzgerald's Park. The discussion turned to cricket and the relative merits of the great Australian Don Bradman and England's premier opening batsman Len Hutton of Yorkshire. I favoured the Englishman over the Australian, but was willing to change my opinion because I knew my father had a contrary view.

'Never be afraid to have an opinion,' he said. 'Never be influenced by others. However unpopular it may be, hold your ground.'

It was then, all those years ago on that Sunday morning, that the George Hook some people see as controversial was created. Every day I broadcast, my father's words are in my head.

This book is about my opinions on who was the best, who was the worst or who was the most exciting. My aim is not for everyone to agree with me but to promote debate and discussion, which is at the very nub of all sporting conversations.

I hope you enjoy the read.

Note on the text

The genesis of some sections of the book is in the many conversations that Hugh Cahill and I have had over the past number of years since he became RTÉ's rugby commentator. I was struck by his extraordinary knowledge of the professional game, its players and coaches. However, when we talk about the amateur era, particularly pre-1980, his knowledge is, as you would expect, from books rather than personal experience. We come from two rugby generations and it set me thinking about the massive changes that have taken place in the game during my lifetime.

Hugh and I argue incessantly about the relative values of the two Grand Slam-winning teams, separated by sixty years, the relative merits of the Lions tours and a lot more besides – and the results of these exchanges are included in this book.

There is a long tradition when rugby people gather – in Ireland or anywhere else – that talk turns to who is the best, the worst, the unluckiest, the oldest, the youngest … Hugh and I have argued and come up with *our* answers. The question is – do you agree?

My topsy-turvy journey to rugby television

The great old cliché that if you work at something you love, you will never work a day in your life has certainly held true for me over the past fifteen years.

Every year, I visit my old school, Presentation College Cork, and talk to the boys of Sixth Year about their futures after the Leaving Certificate. The nub of my argument is about career decisions and the fact that those 550 points do not make medicine the obvious choice, if you want to be a teacher. Too many of our young people today feel that going to college is a vital component of their future and that failing to make the CAO cut-off is a failure that will affect them for the rest of their lives.

In my case, a bad career choice led to thirty years of mental anguish, marriage failure and financial ruin. The decision to become an entrepreneur and run my own business crippled me emotionally and financially and, at the end of that time, I faced losing my wife, my children and my house. Belatedly, I have found happiness because I am doing what I love.

Strangely enough, I had always wanted to be a broadcaster. My father used to take me to rugby games on a Saturday and League of Ireland soccer matches on a Sunday – in those days in Cork, they were all played in the Mardyke. Musgrave Park had not been developed and

Flower Lodge was decades away. My father had an encyclopaedic knowledge of sport and he gave me a love of physical activity that has stayed with me all my life.

However, back to those Saturday afternoons of my childhood watching UCC or Dolphin play rugby and on Sunday looking at Cork Athletic against Shamrock Rovers or Shelbourne. I used to sit in the stand with a soup can on a stick as my microphone and deliver commentaries on the game in front of me, much to the amusement of the people around us. Perhaps they were much more accepting in those far-off days and I wonder if a child trying the same thing at Lansdowne Road today would be hushed up – or indeed would his parents even be there to support him?

Years later, when I went to college, I became friends with Patrick Campbell, the founder of Campbell Catering. We split up after about five years – Pat to become a millionaire and me to head towards failure. However, I digress. Pat and I were friends at college and he had a tape recorder, which he allowed me to borrow. It recorded on large spools of tape and the piece of equipment itself was the size of a modern-day suitcase – in fact, it is doubtful if Michael O'Leary would even allow it in the overhead rack of his aeroplane, such was its size and weight.

But it was a treasure trove to me. I was then about twenty years of age and used to make radio programmes in my bedroom. I did match reports, results sequences and even live commentaries on rugby, soccer and cricket. I mimicked the great voices of the day, Raymond Glendenning on soccer, John Arlott on cricket and Rex Alston on rugby. It gave me endless hours of enjoyment and perhaps if I had met the right kind of adviser, I might have thought about a career in broadcasting.

Instead, like so many young men of my era, I followed the advice of my parents who wanted me to take a safe, pensionable job. Accountants, my mother believed, would always have a job. My father was a clerk at the railway station and, like my mother, had left school at fourteen. For them, an accountancy qualification was the pinnacle of success.

Amazingly, I lacked self-confidence. I never thought I had the talent to appear on radio, nor did I believe that I was good enough to even write a letter of application to the national broadcaster, despite the fact that so many Corkmen had taken the train to Dublin to make careers in broadcasting. The road to my broadcasting career was long and winding with some difficult moments on the way. Having studied accountancy to please my mother, I took a job selling accounting machines, which seemed to merge my skills as a salesman with the accountancy qualification I possessed. I was successful, but a chance meeting with my old college friend Pat Campbell saw me move into the catering business with him.

Our business relationship ended after five years but I continued on by setting up my own company. There is one thing about being an entrepreneur: it is hard and unforgiving if you are

Why I love rugby

Rugby came a little late to me – like all Corkonians, the first ball I played with was a sliotar, in my case on the streets of Albert Road. Late is perhaps an exaggeration as I was seven when I went to Presentation Brothers College and was introduced to rugby.

This sport has been for me a home when I didn't have one, and a refuge when I had. This is the game that has sustained me in my darkest hours and uplifted me in my happy ones. It has been with me all my life and will continue to be that special game that the founding fathers decided on when William Webb Ellis, in defiance of the rules of the time, picked up the ball and ran with it. Long may it continue.

not good at it – and I certainly wasn't very good at it. I struggled on for far too long because I felt I had no alternative.

Rugby kept me sane during that period. I captained most of the teams I was involved with in my late twenties and early thirties. Sadly I discovered my talents as a player too late, but they led me naturally to coaching. The number of teams I have coached is often a topic for after-dinner speakers, but coaching rugby kept me away from the office. I neglected the business I hated to work with rugby teams which I loved. Unfortunately, the former should have paid the bills while the latter should have been a hobby.

The high points in my business life were few and far between but I had coached the USA in the World Cup, Connacht in the interprovincial championship and the Irish students team in the build-up to the first ever Student World Cup.

As an interprovincial coach, I was in close touch with the press corps that covered the games. I was a good interviewee because I could respond in more detail than the usual 'sick as a parrot' and 'over the moon'-type responses, which did not make good copy.

By the time the 1995 Rugby World Cup rolled around, I knew my time at USA Rugby was coming to an end; added to that, things at home hardly gave me much hope of a warm welcome should I return to Ireland on a permanent basis. Then fate took a hand.

Karl Johnston was the rugby writer with the *Irish Press* group of newspapers and he was the first person to suggest that I might have a future in journalism. 'George,' he said, 'you give us journalists all this great information in an interview, why not write it for yourself?' He generously introduced me to the sports editor of the *Sunday Press*, who asked me to write a column for that publication. After three weeks, he asked me if I would consider going to South Africa to cover the 1995 World Cup.

There was one problem. I was not a member of the National Union of Journalists, so I would be on a different expenses regime to Karl and John Redmond, who would also travel to South Africa for the newspaper.

The deal agreed was that I would produce an estimate of my costs, which would be divided by the number of articles I would write over the period of the World Cup, thus giving a fee per article. In this way, I would recoup all my expenses with a reasonable profit. It seemed like a good idea to me – even in my financially straitened circumstances I probably would have scraped enough together to go down to South Africa. Thrilled at the prospect of going to a rugby tournament and being paid for the privilege, I went to my old friend, travel agent Eugene McGee, to make the arrangements.

Excited at the prospect of an expenses-paid trip, I asked him to book me a business-class flight. I can remember exactly how much the total cost was – £5,500 in old money. I consoled myself that I was going to get it all back at the end of the tournament and Eugene, to his everlasting credit, was prepared to wait for payment until I received the money from the newspaper.

So the great adventure began. I flew in the luxury of British Airways business class to Johannesburg, where I was greeted at the arrivals gate by a downcast Karl Johnston. 'George,' said he, 'the paper has gone bust!'

In the space of an aeroplane journey from London to Johannesburg, one of Ireland's great newspapers, founded by Eamon de Valera himself, had shut down.

Here I was, thousands of miles from home to cover a tournament for which I had no employer. I put the debt to my travel agent to the back of my mind and resolved to enjoy the weeks ahead.

The then production manager at RTÉ, John D. O'Brien, was very kind to me and offered me a spot on the pre-match build-up to the final pool game against Wales in Johannesburg. I cannot remember the fee involved, but it was certainly less than £50 and made little inroad into my bill.

The instructions from O'Brien were clear. The interview would take place by the side of

My favourite broadcasting moment

Over the past decade and a half of my work for RTÉ, there have been some wonderful moments. It has always been fun, and I can honestly say that the moment the green light goes on in the studio, I am in a very happy place. I am nervous and stressed before the event happens but once I am working, it is just great to be talking about the game I love in the company of people with whom I am comfortable.

A best moment is hard to choose, but one day does comfortably beat all the other great broadcasting days I have had so far – Cardiff and the 2006 Heineken Cup final between Munster and Biarritz. I flew to Heathrow late the night before the game, after my radio show, and stayed at an airport hotel. Early the following morning, I drove to Cardiff. The rest of the RTÉ team were already in place in the hotel, and we chatted and read the papers until it was time to go to the stadium. Cathal Goan, then director general of RTÉ, was also in the Welsh capital for the game and he joined Tom, Brent and myself for the short walk to the stadium.

Obviously, we were going to be there a couple of hours before the game to prepare, so most of the Munster fans were still milling around Cardiff because the Millennium Stadium is right in the middle of town.

It was a most extraordinary walk to the ground. Something I have never experienced before or since. Almost every step of the way, we were recognised, cheered and photographed. McGurk turned to me and said, 'George, this ought to be worth a pay rise. The director general has never seen his employees treated like this.' It really demonstrated the bond – sometimes positive and sometimes negative, but always generous and good humoured – between the panel and the Munster supporters. It was a fantastic feeling.

The match itself is a matter of record but there were moments that stood out for me. In the first half, Munster were under the cosh and David Wallace, one of the great wing-forwards of the professional era, consistently carried the ball with immense strength and athleticism, to bring his team out of the defensive zone. At times, it seemed as if he was the only player capable of matching the French opposition.

Half-time also remains etched in my memory. There was some musical entertainment provided by a milk-and-water French singer and then Cara O'Sullivan, the great Cork soprano, came to the centre of the field and sang 'Stand Up and Fight' to a packed stadium, dominated by red-jersied Munster supporters. We will never know what the effect was on the Munster team in the dressing room, but they would not have been human if they had not been intensely moved, as I assuredly was in the broadcasting studio.

Then, it seemed on cue, the television director of the world feed threw up on the stadium television the scene of O'Connell Street in Limerick. It seemed the whole population of the city had come to watch the match on big screens. As players returned to the field to the amazing scene pictured above them, I thought that Munster could not be beaten as the tide of emotion was running in their direction.

Obviously we stayed on air for some time after the final whistle to analyse the game, and, by the time we left the stadium, it was deserted. I am not sure why, but for some reason Tom, Brent and myself made our individual ways back to the hotel rather than going as a group as we had arrived. It took me two hours to make it back as every step of the way I was mobbed by celebrating Munster supporters who were engaging in improvised games of touch rugby on the streets of Cardiff. Others were just standing in the streets savouring the incredible emotion and joy of the victory. Many of them had followed Munster on the great odyssey towards this trophy and had seen the cup dashed from their lips on too many occasions.

This was a special day for Munster fans, and it was the day they wanted me to join in the celebrations with them. I signed autographs, had my photograph taken and was hugged by beautiful young women, who rather spoiled the moment by telling me that I was loved by their mother.

I finally arrived at the hotel, feeling like a boxer who had just gone fifteen rounds in the ring. Tom and Brent were there, having had similar experiences. We were all very proud and honoured that we had been treated in that way by the people who watch our work at weekends. It meant a great deal. Sadly, the director general didn't give us a raise – but if our pockets were empty, our hearts were overflowing with joy and pleasure.

the swimming pool with the match commentator Fred Cogley on the morning of the game and the producer was insistent that I had no more than two minutes. I did not see this as an opportunity to make my name in television, but nevertheless I practised assiduously for the interview. I can remember still, in my hotel room that morning, standing in front of the mirror delivering my lines. It went well and was transmitted back to Dublin, where Bill O'Herlihy, who was then in the Tom McGurk role, made a complimentary comment about my efforts.

What happened to the debt to the travel agent? Well, it took me the best part of five years to pay back Eugene McGee, but I am happy to say that we remain friends to this day. However, something else happened as a result of that two minutes of television.

Niall Cogley was in charge of rugby for RTÉ and as he made his plans for the series of international friendlies two seasons later, he remembered my performance in South Africa. He brought me in and I did some analysis for the game against Western Samoa in November, but it was the following January, and the game against Italy, that really set me off on a new career.

As was usual on Saturday afternoons at that time, RTÉ had a lot of sport on their schedule. But as luck would have it, storms broke out across Britain and Ireland, and a huge number of sporting events were cancelled.

Michael Lyster and I were responsible for the rugby. It was a small team because it was thought that there would be little time for analysis. Instead, the many cancellations meant that I was now required to shore up the afternoon's broadcasting. It was an unbelievable opportunity to showcase my talents. Happily for me, it went well and Cogley decided to use me in the Five Nations Championship that season.

At that time, there was a rotating panel, with Brent Pope, Tony Ward, Ralph Keyes and Ciaran Fitzgerald all being used on an ongoing basis. Similarly, the panel often included a former international from the opposing country. I can remember Doddie Weir of Scotland, Philippe Saint-André of France, Matt Dawson of England and Tony Clement of Wales appearing on programmes over the years.

In 1998, the arrival at RTÉ of Glen Killane as rugby editor changed my life forever. Glen in his wisdom decided that he would go with a regular panel of Tom McGurk, Brent Pope and myself. A decision that made me a fully fledged TV pundit.

For the first time in thirty years, I had a regular – if meagre – income. But the psychological boost to my morale of a wages envelope dropping through my letterbox was incalculable. The 'lovely' Ingrid for the first time in three decades saw the man she loved, happy in his work and earning an income.

This move to TV pundit had another unintended consequence. Adamhain O'Sullivan was the sports editor of the *Sunday Independent* and had watched my work. Before the second match in the Five Nations against Wales, he called me and offered me £25 for a column on the game to appear the day after it was played. Part of the deal was that it would be written by a ghostwriter, something I rejected, to Adamhain's surprise. I remember well his reaction when I suggested that I would write it myself.

'Can you do that, George?' he asked.

'I went to school, didn't I?' I replied.

Immediately after the broadcast, I sat down and penned 500 words of my best prose and called it down a telephone line to a waiting typist in Middle Abbey Street. I continued to write for the remaining games in the championship and then was offered an ongoing column at the same rate of pay, providing my efforts were worthy of publication.

I knew I could write, but it was O'Sullivan who taught me the disciplines of journalism. He became an outstanding mentor, teaching me the first principles of 'who, what and where' that should always appear in the first paragraph to set the piece in context. He never accepted less than my best, often referring a piece back to me suggesting I could do better. For the first time in my working life, I had some money and somebody who believed in me and helped me to improve. It is a debt I can never repay.

My contract relationship with O'Sullivan was also interesting in that for over a decade we negotiated every year on the basis of a handshake. In January, he would meet me for a coffee and suggest the amount that he would pay me per article for the following twelve months. I invariably accepted and never had a contract.

Meanwhile, although faces in the management of television have changed at RTÉ, the standards expected in broadcasting have not. The national broadcaster takes its fair share of criticism, much of it justified, but it is a market leader in its sports coverage. The panels in GAA, rugby and soccer have a uniqueness that sets them apart from other television stations, and management in Montrose never tells its panellists how to dress, what to say or to follow a particular line. There are a few advantages to growing old, but one of them certainly applies to television punditry. Even in those early days, seventeen years ago, I resolved not to be a fan, but an analyst. This was difficult when I was watching my beloved Munster or Ireland or indeed any Irish team, but it is necessary. It doesn't make for fun watching but I believe it is crucially important to remain dispassionate about what is happening in front of me.

There are certainties about television sport that make it difficult for the performer. To that end, Bill O'Herlihy was vitally important with his advice to me in the early days. When I started, Bill was carrying an enormous workload. He chaired the panels at soccer and the Olympics as well as rugby. Strangely enough, although we were both from Cork, I didn't know him very well before my early games in the 1997 Five Nations Championship.

He took me aside before the first game and said, 'George, remember that 75 per cent of the

My worst broadcasting moment

RTÉ Studios during the 2011 Rugby World Cup represent the nadir of my career in television, though it could so easily have been another wonderful time to remember.

World championships in any sport pose difficult challenges for a television station. The large number of events to be broadcast requires that substantial numbers of people are involved in production, commentary, reporting and analysis. RWC 2011 in New Zealand was, in fact, only my third such tournament as a television analyst. I had covered 1999 and 2003, but the contract went elsewhere for 2007 in France. This time around, as the competition was held in the southern hemisphere, all the games were broadcast in the early morning back home in Ireland. Because of the multiplicity of live games and the evening review programmes, there was a need for additional manpower in the punditry department.

For the defining pool game against Australia, Frankie Sheahan joined Brent and myself on the panel. Earlier in the week, Frankie and I had had an altercation over a personal matter which had nothing to do with rugby. Quite unprofessionally, I brought my upset with him into the television studio, even though I knew the first rule of broadcasting is that all extraneous matters are left at the studio door.

Through my fault and my fault alone, there was tension in the studio from the moment the broadcast started. However, it reached disastrous levels during the half-time interval. Frankie, probably due to his inexperience, did not realise how we as a team – and remember Brent, Conor and I are almost telepathic in our understanding – handle interruption.

As I was making what I thought was a very important point about the Australian performance, given that the team had lost two of its most crucial players, at hooker and open-side flanker, just before kick-off, I could sense an interruption coming from my left. Inexcusably, I turned my back on Frankie and continued to make my point aggressively to Tom. It was car-crash television, and I was the author of my own misfortune.

Everything I said was delivered badly and therefore misunderstood by the greater proportion of the audience, who felt I was being unfair to Ireland. I, on the other hand,

believed that, as an analyst, I had to remain neutral and deliver an opinion on what I had just seen. I thought Ireland were flattered by their victory, as the pre-match defections had weakened Australia in the most crucial areas of their game.

After the game, Glen Killane, the managing director of television at RTÉ, sent me a text in which he felt I had misjudged the feelings of the audience. Of course he was right, and I was terribly upset and depressed. It was the lowest point of my broadcasting career, compounded by an article in *The Irish Times* by the television reviewer which was the most savage criticism I have ever received of any aspect of my life.

It was irrelevant that a week later when Ireland lost to Wales in the quarter-final, many of the points I had tried to make were proved correct, when most of Ireland was thinking about winning the competition.

I think a less understanding organisation would have sacked me after that performance and the remainder of the tournament was downbeat as I struggled to come to terms with the enormity of my failure.

Happily, I was given a chance to redeem myself and now, with confidence regained, I look forward to World Cup 2015.

audience at big sports events don't understand the minutia of the game. It is your job to keep it simple and speak in the language that the ordinary man can understand. Don't be too technical.'

It is advice that I have never forgotten. Although I did promptly forget it during my second appearance for the Welsh game. At half-time, Bill asked me about Eric Miller, the Irish number eight. 'Bill,' I said, exhibiting all my knowledge of years in rugby, 'Miller has very high cardiovascular endurance.'

Bill put me in my place with a withering response. Accentuated in his Cork accent and acting the role of the spokesman for the plain people of Ireland, he asked, 'What exactly is cardiovascular endurance, George?'

I was mortified and had to explain that it meant that the player was very fit. It was a timely lesson. Don't use big words, don't be overly technical and, above all, don't appear to be a smart ass.

I have never made that mistake again and, in fact, many of my one-liners are created to try and explain, in a short but dramatic way, my feelings on a particular topic – such as when I tried to explain that Reggie Corrigan might perhaps be reaching the end of his career and I famously told McGurk that 'if Reggie's sell-by date was on my yoghurt, there would be trees growing in it'.

I am a firm believer in Mark Twain's adage that it takes three weeks to prepare any worthwhile off-the-cuff remark. So in the build-up to any broadcast, I spend my time talking to myself in the car and rehearsing the broadcast and answering questions from an imaginary Tom McGurk, sitting in the passenger seat. But it is not all rehearsed: in January 2003 when absolutely overcome with emotion at Munster's extraordinary exploits in beating Gloucester against all the odds at Thomond Park, I was moved to compare the famous ground to Lourdes, Fatima and Knock as a place where miracles happen.

Live television is a very stressful activity. Every day as I'm walking into the studio, I am aware that one unfortunate remark could end my career. After all this time, I still assume that the microphones are off during the break, despite the experience of people like Ron Atkinson, who was sacked for a politically incorrect comment when he thought he was off the air. I really should know better.

RTÉ is very generous to its panellists in allowing them to say pretty well whatever they want, within the bounds of good behaviour. It has allowed John Giles, Eamon Dunphy and Pat Spillane to flourish. Two comments stick in my mind as occasions when I could have received a rap on the knuckles from upstairs for breaching reasonable political correctness. I remember Alan Lewis refereeing a game against Italy and all the penalties seemed to be going one way. At half-time, I said, 'Alan Lewis has done more damage to Italy than Mussolini.' On another occasion, when France capitulated in the second half to lose an international that they should have won, I told McGurk, 'That is the biggest French surrender since Adolf Hitler walked down the Champs-Elysées.' Even now as I write, I get goose pimples at what a different employer might have done.

One of the things that worries me, but which I have to put to the back of my mind during a broadcast, is that the coaches, players and referees have families watching the programme, and could be hurt by criticism. If I were to worry about that, then I would say nothing in my analysis, which is a problem that faces recently retired players who make the transition to television. It must be very difficult for them to make adverse comments about their friends.

During Warren Gatland's period in office as Irish coach, I was particularly critical of his performance. During one Six Nations Championship, Brent Pope and I were walking down Lansdowne Road past the Berkeley Court on the way to the ground. It was hours before the actual kick-off, but we were there because we had to cover one of the other Six Nations games that was starting earlier. Coincidentally, the Irish team bus pulled up outside the hotel, and the team and coaches descended just as we walked towards the bus.

It was an uncomfortable moment. Gatland walked by first and ignored me, closely followed by Eddie O'Sullivan and the rest of the players, all studiously looking the other way – except for two Limerick players, Peter Clohessy and Mick Galwey, who stopped and chatted to me on the pavement. Neither of those players had any particular reason to be kind to me, but it was indicative of their attitude and independence.

Conversely, on the Sunday morning after my comment about Alan Lewis' handling of the Italian game, I took my son to play nine holes at Milltown Golf Club. I wandered into the professionals' shop to be greeted by the sight of the recipient of my criticism, buying a packet of tees. I was mortified and didn't know where to look. Lewis to his everlasting credit laughed at himself and invited the two of us to play the round of golf with him; little wonder then that he remains a friend of mine to this day.

When I first started on television, I understood one simple fact about the medium – the television camera, for some strange reason, has the ability to see inside a person, so I decided that I would give my opinion, no matter how unpopular. I believed that the job was not a popularity contest, but rather that I should feel comfortable with my own integrity.

One thing was absolutely certain – in those early years, I didn't win the popularity contest in Munster. As it happened, and for absolutely logical reasons, I predicted on many occasions during the great Heineken Cup runs that they might not win, only to be proved wrong. In some cases, it caused great hilarity, prompting comments like, 'I hope George suggests Munster will lose today, then we will definitely win.'

I also remember commenting unfavourably on Shannon's performance during their glory years as All-Ireland champions and, of course, suggesting that John Hayes, their star prop-forward, couldn't scrummage. During that period, I was asked to be master of ceremonies at a rugby event in Limerick in which all the local clubs took a table. Shannon boycotted the event and, as I stood up to speak, I found myself staring down at an empty table right under my nose. To be fair, we kissed and made up and I have spoken at subsequent fundraising events for Shannon.

However, getting it wrong in those early days had an unintended consequence. It created an aura about the programme so that people tuned in just to find out what we had to say. I remember after another titanic struggle in Thomond Park, and a predictable Munster victory against the odds, that we were doing the broadcast on the gantry barely six feet above the ground. We were surrounded by a chanting crowd, bigger than had ever been seen at such television events in the past. McGurk got upset and started calling for police protection as the gantry rattled and shook under the combined weight of a couple of hundred eager Munster fans. I turned around to Popey and said, 'They would never be here if we got it right every week.'

I will retire happy if 50 per cent of the calls I made on television were correct. There have certainly been times where I have got it wrong, most notably when I suggested that the Italian selection of Mauro Bergamasco at scrum-half was a good idea, something that created hilarity in the studio as the Italian went from bad to worse. My comments about Tommy Bowe's lack of pace are routinely thrown back in my face, particularly when I cross the border. To my mind, and others, Bowe's move to Wales had a remarkable effect on his fitness and his career. And, of course, my belief that Joe Schmidt would not suit Leinster was a catastrophic miscalculation.

However, in my defence, there was a logic to my thoughts and although I certainly called time on Schmidt's career far too early, there were some extenuating circumstances. When Schmidt arrived at Leinster, we pundits did the usual job of trying to interpret what he was saying. It took a while to realise that he was a coach who actually said what he meant.

I massively underestimated that aspect of his character. His early interviews were tentative and low-key, and his team played with none of the élan that was to become the hallmark of his coaching. There was no semblance of the continuity game that Schmidt and Vern Cotter had brought to Clermont Auvergne. I simply expected too much and, used to fifteen years of coaches promising much and delivering little, I was ready to believe that Schmidt would not convert senior players to his way of thinking.

Television punditry is not about getting it right, it is about having an opinion. Like John Giles, I have always believed that to be asked to forecast the result of a game is a nonsense. Forecasting results is the stuff of fortune tellers. The role of the analyst is to suggest what could happen and afterwards explain why it did happen.

If there is one thing that upsets me, it is people saying that I set out to be controversial. The fact that my views do not get universal agreement and are expressed in an attention-grabbing way does not make me controversial. Controversial is setting out to create controversy without truly believing in the subject matter.

Whilst it obviously is good fun to suggest that I always get it wrong, that is not quite accurate. Belatedly, some of my more critical assessments have been proven right. I was the first analyst to point out the failings in the scrummaging technique of John Hayes, the inability of Stephen Ferris to play at open-side, and the passing and defensive weaknesses in Keith Earls' game, as well as the bad throwing technique of Irish hookers.

If those criticisms were negative, then there were also balancing positive contributions. I suggested that Ronan O'Gara was the best fly-half since Ollie Campbell at a time when the young Corkman was not even in the Munster squad, I consistently pushed the cause of David Wallace when he was ignored by Ireland, and recognised Keith Gleeson as the best open-side in the country.

On occasion when I watch our television competitors, I am bemused by the different standards. Sometimes, everybody in the studio is dressed the same and the only difference is the colour of their ties. I do not suggest we are better or worse, we are just different.

I've always resolved to finish my career in television when I felt comfortable that I still had a contribution to make. Analysis of rugby is about drawing conclusions based on what we see, and I am quite certain that I'm still able to judge the performances of individuals, teams and cultures – but I have resolved to leave television at the end of the 2015 Rugby World Cup. It will be a huge wrench, but it is right for a new generation of analysts to take over.

'Putting Robinson
in the centre is like
            putting a Ferrari in
Stephen's Green on
            a Friday evening,
with Luas works going on —
there's just no space.'

George Hook

The things I hate about rugby

1. **Crooked feed at the scrum**

   If the IRB is not prepared to enforce this aspect of the game, then why allow it to remain in the law book? Week in, week out in provincial and international games, scrum-halves are feeding the ball into the second row. In fact on occasion, it looks as if they are rolling the ball directly to the feet of the number eight. It makes a mockery of the set piece and goes against all principles of a fair contest for possession.

   The results have had repercussions way beyond the mere put-in of the ball. If hookers no longer need to strike for possession, the role of the hooker becomes redundant. We are already seeing this, as there is hardly a world-class number two who can actually strike for the ball. The result of non-striking hookers is that possession down channel one, the quickest ball of all, is no longer used in the game. This means that number eights can no longer make devastating breaks off the back of the scrum because the possession is simply too slow. The loss of channel one possession puts weak scrummaging teams at a disadvantage, as the traditional remedy for being underpowered was to strike the ball quickly down the fast channel and get it away as quickly as possible. It is incredible that in a country like Ireland, which has the worst performing scrums of the major nations, no effort has been made to develop this technique. Every week, we see referees penalise off-line throws at the lineout. Perhaps the IRB and the referees can explain how crooked at one set piece is an offence but not at another.

   Having spent £500,000 on a three-year study of the scrum, the International Rugby Board has established new engagement laws at the scrum, with a suggestion that the ball should be put in straight. The referee will now call 'crouch, bind, set' and wait for the scrum to become stable before instructing the scrum-half to put in the ball straight with the call of 'yes nine'. It is expected to reduce impact at the scrum by 25 per cent, thereby making the scrum safer and increase the possibility of them being completed on the first engagement.

   We can but wait and see.

2. Hookers who cannot throw

When the 2013 Lions touring party to Australia was announced, I felt a huge sense of sympathy for Rory Best. The Ulster hooker, having had his best season on the field and showing good leadership skills, had every right to assume that he would make the trip. That he did not make the original selection was entirely due to his failure to hit the target consistently at the lineout during the Six Nations Championship. Because of Dylan Hartley's moment of madness, Best was to make the tour after all with a late call-up. However, he did not make the test side because the weakness that had caused his omission in the first place came back to haunt him. His competitors for the test were only marginally better and throwing to the tail of the lineout was always a risk for the Lions on that tour.

The tragedy for Best and other Irish hookers – like Sean Cronin, Richardt Strauss and Damien Varley – is that the problem could be solved simply and easily in a matter of weeks. In American football, there is a move called the 'long snap' whereby the ball is thrown between the legs of the snapper to the catcher and placed on the tee for a kicker taking a field goal. It requires speed and accuracy of a very high order. Simply transpose the action from a bent-over position to an upright one and the exact same technique could be used. Dan Rooney, the former US ambassador to Ireland, is the owner of the Pittsburgh Steelers football team. There is no doubt that he would make available one of his coaches to the IRFU to solve its most grievous problem. What is incredibly annoying is that coaches in Ireland who spend hours fixing problems in every other part of the pitch are simply unwilling or unable to solve a simple problem like throwing in at the lineout which very often can decide the result of the match and, in the case of Rory Best, a lifetime's ambition.

3. The interminable continuity game

The legendary Father Hampson of Blackrock College always told his team, 'If we win two consecutive quick rucks, we will score; if we win three consecutive quick rucks, the scrum-half will score.' That was, of course, in the era when rucking in Ireland was in its infancy and, more importantly, when all sixteen forwards committed themselves to the breakdown. Today, the defenders will often only put one or two players in

the ruck and, in the case of South Africa, they do not contest the breakdown at all. This makes it comparatively easy for teams to win successive rucks. Very often, only the speed of delivery is an issue as the 'Groundhogs' like Richie McCaw of New Zealand, David Pocock of Australia and Brian O'Driscoll of Ireland slow down the ball. Munster demonstrated on numerous occasions in their golden era that when in search of a drop goal for Ronan O'Gara or to close out a game, as against Toulouse in the Heineken Cup, the men in red could deliver in excess of forty successful rucks.

Many people, when looking at videos of games played in the 1950s and 1960s, are appalled at the stop–start nature of the game, the inability to win the throw cleanly at the lineout and the large number of scrums awarded. The question is whether the modern game is actually more attractive. Whether it is better to have thirteen defenders strung out in the line across the field as the attackers continue a policy of the scrum-half passing to the nearest team-mate who then crashes in to the nearest body to set up another ruck. The administrators face a difficult problem. There are aspects of the game that are certainly better, notably the lineout, but it will be difficult to persuade a neutral watcher that forty-six rucks is an attractive proposition. There is one other unfortunate side-effect of the modern continuity game – there are now more head-on tackles than ever before with almost certainly long-term damaging effects to the bodies of the players.

4. The demise of clubs

The latest suggestion from the IRFU to try and arrest the diminishing involvement of clubs in Irish rugby and address the dangers of under-the-counter payments to players, is that clubs no longer pay the players and revert to a completely amateur status. Before the advent of professionalism, amateur rugby clubs were fielding anything up to a dozen sides every weekend. Now after a decade and a half of pay for play, some of the great clubs of Ireland are struggling to field three teams. The drop in revenue has been catastrophic as pavilion members are a thing of the past and players are reluctant to pay subscriptions. The result is that sponsorship and the sale of international tickets are the primary revenue sources for Irish rugby. The standard of club play is a long way below that of twenty years ago, as the players involved do not have the talent to progress to representative level and all the players, because of work commitments, marriage or commuting time, are no longer interested in playing into their thirties. Irish rugby simply cannot afford to lose more than a hundred of its top players to provincial squads and academies. The suggestion that clubs should stop paying players is nonsense. A sponsor, who has put a substantial amount of money into a club that is faced with the threat of relegation, is bound to attempt to keep or recruit an outstanding player to protect the investment. Commercial realities will always trump the ideals of the IRFU. Irish club rugby has gone too far down the route of semi-professionalism to turn back now.

5. The treatment of Connacht

This year, I watched many of Connacht's games in the RaboDirect Pro12. I was astonished at the standard of play and thought it compared unfavourably with the province's best teams in the amateur era. There is no doubt in my mind that prop-forwards like Tom Clancy, Davy Henshaw and others were superior to the current breed, who are paid for their efforts.

The problem dates back to the decision by the IRFU to scrap Connacht as a professional team. It was the correct decision, but because of public protest, the decision was reversed and, sadly, the province was reduced to development status. That was the wrong decision, and it should never have been accepted by the powers-that-be west of the Shannon. The result has been an underfunded squad full of average players, struggling because of the departure of its best players to other provinces. The situation is now beyond repair and the team will continue to struggle as the poor relation of Irish rugby.

6. **Dietary supplements for schoolboy rugby players**
Over ten years ago, I wrote about the dangers of food supplements for schoolboys. It created a short-term scandal when the paper's research discovered that many of the top schools' rugby teams in Ireland were routinely prescribing food supplements of doubtful provenance to their players. Since then, countless doctors have warned of the dangers of products sold over-the-counter without proper labelling of the ingredients or supervision by the Irish Medicines Board. A loophole in the regulatory laws allows food supplements to bypass the stringent testing that would normally be applied to pharmaceutical products. Despite reports that there may be connections between sudden death syndrome in young adults and overdoses of supplements, schools rugby players are still routinely using these products in the quest to become bigger. The outstanding example given by Gordon D'Arcy has never received the publicity it deserved. When the Irish centre was on the Lions tour to New Zealand, he refused to take any products that were not sufficiently labelled and thereby regulated. He should be used by the IRFU in an advertising campaign, warning young people of the dangers of the indiscriminate use of food supplements.

7. **The rugby academies**
Only a minority of participants in sport turn professional. An even smaller minority are financially successful. The problem for rugby, unlike soccer or golf, is that even at

the top level, rugby players do not earn enough money to enable them to stop working when they retire. So, when they do finish playing, they are faced with the difficulty of seeking work while having neither qualifications nor experience to interest an employer. Today, the state of the economy precludes companies from hiring 'poster boys' with no skills. The difficulty is multiplied for the young man who gives up the opportunity to learn a trade or profession in the hope of making the big-time of professional rugby. The example of Padraig Harrington is instructive. He trained as an accountant before turning professional to ensure that if he failed as a professional golfer, he had a worthwhile qualification. The other failure of the academies is that the members do not associate with retired players who could advise them on the future. It is hard to believe that the current 'force feeding' of young rugby aspirants is superior to the club structure it replaced.

8. Tag Rugby

This year, with great fanfare, the IRFU announced that more and more people are playing Tag Rugby — in Ireland, the number is currently about 20,000 — and that women make up nearly 50 per cent of the total. This is great news for the statisticians when they talk about the number of people involved in the game — the reality, however, is very different. Tag has as much to do with rugby as swords and spears do with modern warfare. Obviously, there is a great attraction to a sport that has no physical collisions and has the added advantage of creating a social environment for men and women to mix. The tragedy is that it ensures that a large number of people are not involved in the club game in Ireland. If every one of the participants were members of a rugby club, it would probably inject €2 million into the club game in subscriptions alone and, more importantly, identify talent for the fifteen-a-side game.

9. The great concussion debate

'Good news doesn't sell newspapers': this is a long-held view and perhaps explains why the headlines in our newspapers are invariably full of depressing economic figures, scandals about celebrities or the failures of our sporting heroes. It is surprising, therefore, that a story filling the pages of American newspapers, and not just the sports pages, has never crossed the Atlantic. Former footballers are now suing the NFL for brain damage as a result of repeated concussions received while they were players. The medical profession and the IRFU have failed to grasp this nettle. The supposed 'concussion bin' was to give doctors the opportunity to check out the health of a player, whom they could only allow back on the field if he was clearly fit to play, with no obvious danger signs for the future. However, almost from the off, the plan lost all credibility for anybody watching the Ireland–Argentina game in the Aviva in November 2012. The Argentinian scrum-half was led off clearly not knowing which end was up. Yet, within minutes he returned to the fray. And then, far more worryingly, in 2013 we saw Luke Marshall concussed, to return a week later only to be concussed again and then unbelievably he was allowed to return to the fray to be concussed a third time. It may not be the end of his rugby career, but it is deeply worrying. I cannot challenge the medical experts on what is or is not concussion but, as a former player, a former coach, a former parent and a still-committed watcher of rugby union, it is obvious that many Irish players have suffered some kind of brain trauma during rugby games and have been allowed to continue.

The answer is not how they feel after the game, or indeed how they feel at the end of their careers. What American footballers have discovered is that well into their retirement, they are suffering with a whole raft of serious side-effects because of their active participation in sport. Some players have even donated their brains to medical science to help the case against the governing bodies of the major physical contact sports and force them to look into this problem. Realistically, we will not get action until the parents of schoolchildren start making a stand by switching codes for their sons and daughters. That is what happened in New Zealand after there were a large number of catastrophic injuries in the scrum. The NZRFU, frightened by young people drifting away from their sport, brought in the under-19 variation at the scrum. We need immediate and strong action by the International Rugby Board, but I will not be holding my breath. Professional sportsmen have always been pawns in the great world of sporting commerce.

this is
Rugby

3 GREAT LANSDOWNE MOMENTS

1. 1956

This was a very special year and a very special match, as it marked my first visit to Lansdowne Road. Living in Cork, and with the family short of money, the opportunities for me to get to Dublin, despite my father having free tickets on the train as a railway employee, were pretty slim.

I was ecstatic when my father came home from work one Thursday holding tickets for the game against Wales the following Saturday. In those days, international tickets

Noel Henderson leads Ireland out from the old Lansdowne RFC clubhouse in front of the open Havelock Square End.

could also be bought in Lawson's outfitters in McCurtain Street in Cork and he had got his hands on two of the elusive pieces of pasteboard.

The trip started when an early-morning train from Cork transported me to the sophistication of Dublin. The proliferation of traffic lights on the journey from Heuston Station, then known as Kingsbridge, to the city centre was an adventure in itself.

More firsts awaited. My father bought me beans on toast followed by a Knickerbocker Glory in Cafolla's ice-cream parlour on O'Connell Street. We took a booth because on the wall there was a machine that operated the jukebox, a mechanism I'd only previously read about in comic books. One coin excitedly pushed into the slot brought the strains of Guy Mitchell and 'Singing the Blues' over the sound system.

We went to the ground early to get a good spot as we were going to be standing on the terraces. The walk along Lansdowne Road and over the level crossing has never been bettered – no programme was ever read with such rapt concentration and no other Irish team has made my heart beat more than the one led out by Noel Henderson on that magical March afternoon.

Wales were coming in search of the Triple Crown and seemingly unbeatable by an Irish side that had performed poorly in the three games up to this match. However, crucial changes had been made for the Scotland game that had been won. The great Paddy Berkery was at full-back, a selection that cheered everybody in Munster, and Kyle and O'Meara were reunited at half-back.

Ireland were simply magnificent and Welsh ambitions were destroyed by a rampaging Irish back row led by Corkman Marnie Cunningham, who retired from rugby soon after with a late vocation to the priesthood.

The highlight of the afternoon was the first and, as it turned out, only drop goal in Jackie Kyle's forty-six-cap career for Ireland. I was high on the terraces at the Havelock Square End, but behind the goalposts that were in fly-half's sights. The great Ulsterman kicked high and true from forty yards out and on the touchline in front of the East Stand.

After that, Ireland were never going to be beaten and one very happy but tired young man went home on the train full of stories to tell his classmates the following Monday.

2. 1973

The 1972 championship was disrupted by political rather than sporting decisions. Ireland opened with two away wins in Paris and London and with Scotland and Wales due to come in Lansdowne Road, hopes were high of a record-breaking season.

Sadly it was not to be.

The Scottish captain Peter Brown was reputedly threatened by the IRA and he influenced his team-mates, and ultimately the Scottish Rugby Union, and they refused to travel to Dublin. The Welsh duly followed suit.

It was a disaster for the championship, and fears that England might not travel the following year were worrying.

On taking office for the 1972–1973 season, Dickie Kingswell, the new president of the RFU, declared in his acceptance address that England would fulfil their fixture in Dublin. And travel they did.

It is hard at a distance of forty years to imagine how people felt about an English team coming to Dublin when there were, seemingly, threats to their lives. The gardaí were magnificent and it was their assurances coupled with those of the IRFU that satisfied all doubts in England.

As kick-off time approached on 10 February 1973, the atmosphere was electric. The English team ran onto the field, led by their captain John Pullin, from the old Lansdowne FC clubhouse at the Havelock Square End. They were greeted by the band playing the 'British Grenadiers' and then, in a marketing master-stroke, the IRFU left the English team warming up on the pitch for a full five minutes while 55,000 people stood and applauded for the entire time. No English team in any sport has ever received such a reception in Ireland.

I watched it from high in the West Stand with my father, and I can honestly say that there were tears in my eyes. It was a very special moment for Irish rugby, the championship and the gardaí.

As expected, the match passed off without incident and Ireland crowned the day with a victory, 18–9, prompting the English captain to declare in his speech at the post-match dinner, 'We may not be very good, but at least we turn up.'

The stirring Irish opening to the 1973 championship did not translate into the next two games when we were beaten by Scotland and Wales before beating France in Lansdowne Road in the final match.

'We may not be
very good,
but at least
we turn up.'

John Pullin, England captain, 1973

3. 1982

Ireland went into this championship with low expectations. The team was coached by Tom Kiernan and although the 'old silver fox' had masterminded Munster's victory over the All Blacks in 1978, he had now overseen seven consecutive losses by the national team. In those seven games, Ireland had used four fly-halves – Ollie Campbell, Tony Ward, Paul Dean and Mick Quinn. The previous season there had also been the failed experiment of playing two fly-halves in the same backline by moving Campbell to centre, outside Ward.

In November 1981, Ireland had lost to Australia in Lansdowne Road when the back play had been feeble. For the visit of Wales in the first match of the 1982 championship, Kiernan had reverted to the experiment of playing two pivots in the backline, but this time putting Campbell in what was undoubtedly his best position of fly-half and Dean in the centre where his lack of a kicking game would not be exposed.

Campbell was magnificent in the victory over Wales and when England were defeated a fortnight later in Twickenham, a Triple Crown match against Scotland was set up on 20 February – two days after the general election.

The election had unintended consequences for me. All of the RTÉ cameras and crews were around the country for the election coverage and the station was unable to provide the technical backup for the game. BBC Northern Ireland stepped into the breach and provided the broadcast facilities. Unlike RTÉ, the BBC unions required on-site catering. At that time, I was in the location catering business and had done lots of work for BBC Northern Ireland, so they asked me to provide the same services in the stadium. Needless to say I was delighted, as it meant I would be able to watch the game. Tickets were like gold dust and many of my friends had been unable to get any. There was a simple solution. The catering trucks would be entering the ground early in the morning, and no caterer has ever had a bigger crew for an event – more than half the personnel were there just to watch the match.

At that time, I was also coaching the under-19 team at Old Belvidere RFC and the fly-half, Mick Killeen, lived on Lansdowne Road across from the turnstiles. So I was faced with the problem of getting Mick and his pals into the ground without tickets. We arrived at a simple solution where Mrs Killeen equipped the boys with kettles and we marched to the gate with me in the lead waving my caterer's pass and we all got in.

The result of the match against Scotland is a matter of historical record, but I was never again asked to do the catering at Lansdowne Road.

RUGBY *1987* WORLD CUP

The Rugby World Cup of 1987 was pretty special for the game in general and for me in particular. The International Rugby Board with just eight members had seemed an unlikely organisation to develop a world championship.

There was no qualification for that inaugural competition and as South Africa were banned because of the apartheid regime, the seven remaining IRB members decided to invite nine other countries to make up the sixteen-team competition – astonishingly, Western Samoa were omitted as Argentina, Fiji, Italy, Canada, Romania, Tonga, Japan, Zimbabwe and the United States all accepted invitations to make up the numbers.

In 1986, I had presented the USA Rugby national coaching course in Lawrence, Kansas, and had struck up a strong relationship with the Eagles' coach Ron Mayes, who asked me to assist in preparing the American team for the World Cup. It was an astonishing honour for me and typical of the generous California-based Kiwi.

When I travelled to Brisbane for the opening match, I had three favourite countries in my mind. Obviously, I wanted the USA to do well. I was also, as an Irishman, hoping for an outstanding performance from a side that had won the Triple Crown just two years before under Mick Doyle and I wanted Australia to win the tournament outright because of the innovative back play developed by coach Alan Jones.

Twenty-five years ago, the competition had none of its modern-day appeal. The games in Australia were played at Ballymore in Brisbane and the Concord Oval in Sydney. Both grounds had a capacity of about 20,000 and yet they were never sold out for any match, including Australia's home games up to the semi-final stage.

Most of the games in the pool stages ended in easy victories for the major countries, with New Zealand twice scoring over seventy points against Fiji and Italy, while France had a facile 70–12 victory over Zimbabwe, who earlier had let in sixty points against Scotland. The quarter-final line-up was predictable, with Fiji joining the seven IRB member countries.

Ireland arrived at the competition without a coach or an anthem. Mick Doyle suffered a suspected heart attack on the plane and manager Syd Millar took over the coaching. Finding an anthem proved more problematic. This was a time before 'Ireland's Call' – Irish teams had never had to stand for 'Amhrán na bhFiann' when they played abroad because one of the traditions of the game at that time was that only the anthem of the home country was played – but the anthems of both countries would be played in this inaugural World Cup. In the build-up to the first test match against Wales, a political row broke out as to why the anthems should be used in the first place, but a compromise was reached and the search began for a cassette tape to play before games.

Most of the squad had invested in a cassette player so that they could listen to music on the long-haul flight to New Zealand. As one can imagine, the choice of music was eclectic and Phil Orr had bought a cassette of a James Last concert in Kerry, which contained his rendition of the 'Rose of Tralee'. It was decided to use the tune, but the Unionists back home may have been unaware that the concert had been held in the football stadium named after the revolutionary, hunger striker and IRA man, Austin Stack.

For the first and vital match against Wales the men in green stood for a meaningless song conducted by German bandleader. Meanwhile their opponents were fired up by the great traditional anthem, 'Land of my Fathers'. In the stand, Jim Glennon an Irish reserve turned to manager Syd Millar and said, 'That's a three-point start to Wales.'

It led to the immortal comment by Con Houlihan, 'We used God Save the Rose of Tralee!'

Ireland were nothing like the side that had been so successful just two seasons earlier. They lost to Wales in the pool stages and were given a fright by Canada, who looked like causing an upset with twenty minutes to go, although Ireland eventually ran out comfortable winners.

Ireland predictably lost to Australia in the quarter-final and little did we realise at that time that this level would be the summit of Irish ambitions for the next quarter of a century in this competition.

While Ireland were playing in New Zealand, the US Eagles had the unenviable task of

David Campese of Australia was kept scoreless by Gary Hein of the US Eagles.

facing Australia and England in their pool games. However, the draw worked out favourably for the rookie nation as Japan were first up in Ballymore. It was always recognised that a victory in this match would be an outstanding performance.

In a nail-biting finish, the Eagles won 21–18 and my first venture as an international coach had ended in success. It would be sixteen years before the Eagles' won another game in the Rugby World Cup.

Meanwhile back in Ireland, the games were not being screened live but were watched tape delayed. This time was very much a low point in my life, and I had travelled without telling my wife where I was going. The first she knew about where I was was when she saw me on television for the Japan game.

One surprising feature of the American team was that nobody knew all the words of 'The Star-Spangled Banner' and at the team meeting on the eve of the Japan game, time was devoted to the players learning the words of their national anthem.

The Eagles' second game was against pre-tournament favourites Australia, and the coaching staff took the decision to play the second team in that match and go for broke against England in Sydney four days later. Although the Australians won comfortably, the

'Subdue and penetrate.'

American reserves put on an astonishing fight, which so impressed their opponents that the Australian team came to the changing room en masse after the game to exchange kit as a token of their regard for the rookies.

The performance of many of the players in that match demonstrated that the Eagles' selection system was flawed, caused primarily by the vast distances in the country, which affected the coaches' ability to see players on a regular basis.

Four days later, the Eagles faced England in the final pool game. Morale in the England camp was very low, predicated by the quirky decision of the RFU to pick an oddly assorted management. The coach, Cambridge graduate and school teacher Martin Green, and the assistant coach, the hard-nosed, cloth-capped Lancastrian Dave Seabrook, seemed to be barely on speaking terms. The party was managed by Mike Weston who adopted a completely hands-off approach.

To this day, I believe that with a different selection, the Eagles might well have pulled off a massive surprise or at the very least run England close. The match would turn on the failure of the American scrum to compete, a weakness that had been identified months before.

The final games of the pool were played in Sydney and the US and Australia squads were on the same flight from Brisbane. Ron Mayes approached Alan Jones about the possibility of getting some scrum practice the day before the vital game against England.

The ebullient Jones replied, 'I will do better than that, mate, I will send my reserve pack and coach to your practice.'

It was an astonishing gesture and I doubt it has ever been seen before or since in international rugby. Sadly, the last-minute practice did not bear fruit but Alan Jones remains at the very top of my list of favourite coaches.

Although they beat the Eagles, England departed the tournament in the quarter-final after losing tamely to Wales.

Australia were to lose in the dying seconds of the semi-final against France when a magnificent Serge Blanco try won the game for his team. Jones will certainly go to his grave lamenting the failure of the referee to pick up a knock-on and two forward passes in the build-up to the winning score. However, the try remains one of the great moments in World Cup history.

France were comfortably beaten in the final by New Zealand but when the captain Dave Kirk held the cup aloft, nobody imagined that it would be twenty-four years before another New Zealander would repeat the achievement.

Campbell V Ward

There has always been talk of a Welsh fly-half conveyor belt, but in Ireland over the past sixty years or more, there have been periods when the country has been blessed with two outstanding contenders for the number ten shirt.

In the 1950s as Jack Kyle's career was drawing to a close, many people thought that Seamus Kelly of Lansdowne should be selected. Ten years later, the Irish selectors shoe-horned two outstanding fly-halves in to the same backline when they selected Mike Gibson in the centre with Barry McGann in the pivotal role.

In more recent years, Ronan O'Gara has had to contend with the competing claims of David Humphreys and Jonny Sexton. All three have been outstanding performers for Ireland and each has a substantial cohort of support, convinced that their man was best.

However, the most divisive fly-half debate revolves around two players with completely different styles and personalities. Seamus Oliver Campbell was first capped against Australia at Lansdowne Road in 1976, while Anthony Joseph Patrick Ward made his debut in 1978 in the first match of the Five Nations Championship at home against Scotland.

Campbell's scrum-half against Australia was another debutant, John Robbie. The youngsters were good friends and had been outstanding for Leinster. However, that day in January 1976 was not outstanding for either man – after it, Campbell was dropped and Robbie only survived for one more game.

It was a period when the Irish selectors did not seem to know who was the best number ten. For the next eight games, they picked three fly-halves – Barry McGann, Mike Gibson and Mick Quinn. To complicate matters further, there seemed to be no dedicated place-kicker and the duties were shared between Robbie, McGann, Gibson and Quinn.

Tony Ward, who had been to St Mary's College in Dublin, was a student at what is now the University of Limerick and playing his rugby at Garryowen. In his first match for Ireland, he kicked two penalty goals and a conversion. Ireland lost the next three games in the 1978 Five Nations, but Ward ended the season with an impressive tally of thirty-eight points.

He was an instant hit with spectators with his impressive kicking, his darting, jinking runs and his handsome good looks. The following year, Ireland's season consisted of one win, two draws and two losses, but Ward racked up another twenty-seven points and won the Golden Boot award for European rugby. It seemed he could do no wrong.

Meanwhile Campbell had been playing very little club or provincial rugby because of a troublesome hamstring injury, but he proved his fitness in the Leinster Senior Cup campaign of 1979 and accompanied Ward on the short Irish tour to Australia that summer.

As the man in possession, Ward had every expectation of being the starting number ten for the two test matches. However, in a dramatic selection decision, manager Jack Coffey, coach Noel Murphy and captain Fergus Slattery decided to select Campbell for the first test.

It was a bombshell for the supporters back home and a catastrophic blow to Ward's self-esteem. Campbell had a magnificent match in the 27–12 victory in Brisbane. He was naturally retained for the second test, when Ireland won again.

However, despite being part of the most successful Ireland overseas tour in history, Campbell's position was not secure either. Ireland was divided, and nowhere was the division more obvious than amongst the press corps. *The Irish Times* devoted an entire page to the argument. Never before or since has so much space in a national newspaper been given to a selection decision between two players. But all the coverage simply added fuel to the flames.

Campbell was selected for the entire 1980 Five Nations Championship and against France in the opening game of the 1981 series. Throughout that period, there had been a consistent campaign for the selection of Ward and Campbell in the same backline. The Irish selectors succumbed to the pressure and, for the remaining three games of the 1981 season, they selected Campbell in the centre with Ward at fly-half. It was of little avail as Ireland failed to win a match.

The Lions toured South Africa in 1980 and lost an incredibly close test series 3–1 but Campbell and Ward were both selected, along with scrum-halves John Robbie and Colin Patterson. Campbell was selected for two tests and Ward for one. Welshman Gareth Davies played in the other test.

For many people, the defining match in the debate was a game against Australia in Lansdowne Road in November 1981. Ireland lost 16–12 but the view was that the backline failed to function with Ward at fly-half.

Coach Tommy Kiernan, who had now overseen seven successive defeats, made a change at number ten to bring back Campbell. It was to be an inspired choice as Campbell had the season of his life and masterminded a Triple Crown for Ireland.

The highlights were his blindside break to set up a Moss Finn try against Wales; his incredible touchline conversion to win the match against England at Twickenham and, of course, his twenty-one-point haul in the final game against Scotland.

Ireland were denied a Grand Slam by France in Paris and the following year only a defeat by Wales in Cardiff prevented another winning season. Subsequently, Campbell was picked to go to New Zealand on a Lions tour under manager Willie John McBride, coach Jim Telfer and captain Ciaran Fitzgerald. It was neither a successful nor a particularly happy tour and Campbell never seemed completely happy with his lot.

The British press vilified Fitzgerald and cast doubts on Campbell's fitness to be the first choice fly-half. Many considered that Scotsman John Rutherford would have been a better choice. Jim Telfer was never happy in an Irish-dominated trio and felt excluded. The tough Scotsman was to have his valediction in the successful Lions tour of South Africa in 1997.

Campbell returned from the tour to play in the first three games of the 1984 Five Nations before being replaced by his old adversary Ward for the final two games. That season was not satisfactory for either of them, as Ireland lost every game, which led to the appointment of Mick Doyle as coach for the following season. Campbell never played for Ireland again.

In a complete change, the new coach went for Paul Dean as his number ten and encouraged him to develop his 'give it a lash' philosophy. It worked and Ireland won another Triple Crown, though Ward won three more caps, including two at the 1987 World Cup when he was the backup to Paul Dean.

Twenty-five years later, the debate still goes on amongst people who watched rugby at that time. Everybody, whether rugby expert or not, had an opinion. Campbell tells the story of giving a lift to an old lady when he was driving on a business trip to Mayo. Rugby came up in the conversation and his passenger said, 'I know nothing about rugby but I think it is awful the way they treat that young man, Tony Ward.'

On balance, Campbell takes the palm by virtue of his superior passing skills and the ability to bring the best out of an attacking backline. He was also a better defender than Ward. However, both were outstanding goal-kickers and in their different ways outstanding ambassadors for the game.

Irish women's rugby is on a high following the Six Nations Grand Slam of 2013. This fantastic achievement came after a quarter-final appearance in the 2010 World Cup, having beaten perennial heavyweights the USA en route. In 2013, they also achieved eighth place in the Sevens World Cup in Moscow, having toppled another major nation, South Africa, in the pool stages and were within two minutes of victory over the USA in the quarter-final. Their success has its own problems in that the same players are asked to perform in sevens and the full game, including Lynne Cantwell, Ireland's most capped player. Their recent success puts an Olympic place in sight, which will attract top-class athletes from other sports.

Little did Eddie O'Sullivan and I imagine when we were asked to coach the first Irish women's squad for the inaugural, if unofficial, World Cup in 1991 that such success would follow. No doubt today's players will remember those early pioneering women who faced criticism and derision from many who should have known better.

Which Irish Grand Slam team was the best?

Ireland's two Grand Slams are separated by sixty years, which makes them difficult to compare. Comparisons are made even more difficult because one team was amateur and the other professional. And for people unfamiliar with the immediate post-war period, it is difficult to comprehend the hardships that the population of Europe was suffering even though the war had ended almost three years earlier.

Ireland's last pre-war game was a loss to Wales as Ravenhill on 11 March 1939. At that point, France had been banned for the previous eight years because of allegations of professionalism, so it was a Four Nations Championship. There was to be no more formal international rugby until January 1947, when Ireland hosted a rejuvenated France at Lansdowne Road.

The team contained two Second World War veterans in prop J.C. Daly and flanker Bill McKay. Sadly both flankers from the 1939 game – Herbert Sayers and Robert Alexander – were killed during the conflict and second row Blair Mayne had had to retire because of war injuries.

Con Murphy of Lansdowne, as the only survivor from the pre-war match, was the captain of the team as his fourteen team-mates had never played in an international before. In that season, Ireland beat England and Scotland but lost to France and Wales.

At the beginning of the 1947–1948 season, Australia came to Dublin and beat Ireland 16–3. However, the match was vital as it gave the team a chance to settle. That match was significant for the selection of Kevin O'Flanagan on the wing, which made him a dual international at rugby and soccer. His brother Mick was to play against Scotland and also had the distinction of playing international rugby and soccer.

Until 1973, the games in the championship followed the same pattern. France were first up on the list followed by England, Scotland and Wales. In the late 1940s, because of France's long absence from the championship, the Triple Crown was seen as being more important than the Grand Slam. Thus, France were seen as something of a pipe-opener and, for the next thirty years, Wales was Ireland's bogey team on many occasions when a Triple Crown beckoned.

Travel was difficult and the trek to Paris was by boat and train. On the day, both sides scored two tries but the Irish victory was secured by wing Barney Mullan kicking two conversions. The match was significant for the arrival of new cap Jim McCarthy from Dolphin, who was just over twelve stone but was the quintessential open-side flanker. Such was his rapport with the fly-half's that he became known as Jackie Kyle 'dispatch rider'.

Next up was England at Twickenham whose record in total, but particularly at headquarters, was vastly superior to Ireland. In an eerie coincidence with 2009, Ireland were to win by a single point. Kyle was magnificent at fly-half and capped his performance with a try. The teak-tough Bill McKay did what he was to do so often for the Lions two years later, and crossed the try line.

Ireland now faced two home games to succeed where few had gone before. Scotland put up a tough fight but, once again, Kyle was in supreme form and scored another try. Mullan, whose poor kicking could so easily have let the side down, also contributed a try for a famous six-point victory.

The biggest day in Irish rugby history was set for 13 March 1948 at Ravenhill in Belfast. The Northern capital might not have suffered as London had in the war, but food rationing and other emergency measures had made life difficult for the Ulster players. Jim McCarthy remembered how the players from the south of Ireland would invariably pack their kitbags with bacon and sausages for their mates in Northern Ireland. Even that simple task was not that easy because there were eagle-eyed customs officers on both sides of the border ready to confiscate any contraband.

The match was nip and tuck the whole way through, and Mullan scored another try for Ireland but Wales levelled with a try of their own. The match was won by prop-forward J.C. Daly who crossed for the winning score. Daly's remark went down in history: 'Jaysus, after this, we will all be canonised.'

J.C. Daly of Ireland crawls out of a scrum with the ball during Ireland's Grand Slam-winning match against Wales in Belfast.

The players were overwhelmed by the supporters and most had their jerseys torn to shreds as people tried to get a souvenir of the great occasion. The players were largely unaware of the magnitude of their achievement and as the surviving members were all to say in 2009, they never imagined that it would be sixty-one years before their achievement was equalled.

Why do I consider the 1948 Grand Slam to be superior to the 2009 performance? The issue of pay for play is not relevant because the training and conditioning were similar for the respective opponents. However, certain comparisons can be made.

First and foremost, the 1948 team scored ten tries but only converted three, in marked contrast to the success rate of the modern era. In four games, they did not kick a single penalty goal. The dominance of the goal-kicker was not to be seen for decades to come. Ronan O'Gara kicked fifty-one points in 2009, while Barney Mullan kicked just six points in 1948.

The 2009 side scored just seven tries but converted six, as well as kicking nine penalty goals and three drop goals. Arguably, the team of 1948 was a better attacking side. Interestingly, Jim McCarthy scored seven tries in a career covering twenty-eight appearances, a strike rate unparalleled for an open-side flanker. In comparison, Fergus Slattery scored just three tries in sixty appearances for Ireland.

Secondly, this team contained all the vital selection ingredients to be a great side. They had a dominant fly-half, the best in the world, backed up by an outstanding back row. It is interesting that the successful teams that were to follow them all had strength in those crucial areas.

Thirdly, like all great teams, they possessed a superb captain in Karl Mullen. The young medical student was a leader, a tactician and a motivator who was to be recognised when he was awarded the captaincy of the Lions tour to New Zealand in 1950.

The role of the forwards in the engine room has often been underestimated. This team had two tough operators in Jimmie Nelson and Colm Callan. Nelson proved just how tough he was with his later performances for the Lions.

The key tactical differences were that in the 1948 Grand Slam, forward play was crucial. At the scrum, the hooker struck on the opposing put-in which often created a surplus of possession.

Similarly, the number eight often kept the ball at his feet and the back row 'wheeled' off the scrum in a fearsome 'foot rush'. The control in the dribble was important and woe-betide the opponent who went to ground at the feet of the onrushing forwards.

The ruck was unknown as the tackled player had to play the ball with his boot before continuing the movement. Multi-phase rugby was unknown and if three consecutive possessions were achieved, a try was nearly certain.

The role of the number ten was different too. In attack, Kyle was likely to break the line or set up a score for a team-mate. In defence, there was no head-on tackling, rather the fly-half headed for the corner flag as a last line of defence.

Using modern scoring methods and assuming similar kicking skills, the 1948 team would have scored over a hundred points in a Six Nations Championship today. Kyle would have been a hero of the twenty-first century as he was of the twentieth. The back row of McCarthy, Bill McKay and Des O'Brien would have been a marauding trio.

I suspect that the men of 2009 would have found it more difficult to go back in time than the heroes of 1948 would have to fast forward sixty years.

1948 TEAM:

Dudley Higgins; Bertie O'Hanlon, Des McKee, Paddy Reid, Barney Mullan; Jack Kyle, Ernie Strathdee; Jackie Daly, Karl Mullen, Albert McConnell; Jimmie Nelson, Colm Callan; Bill McKay, Des O'Brien, Jim McCarthy

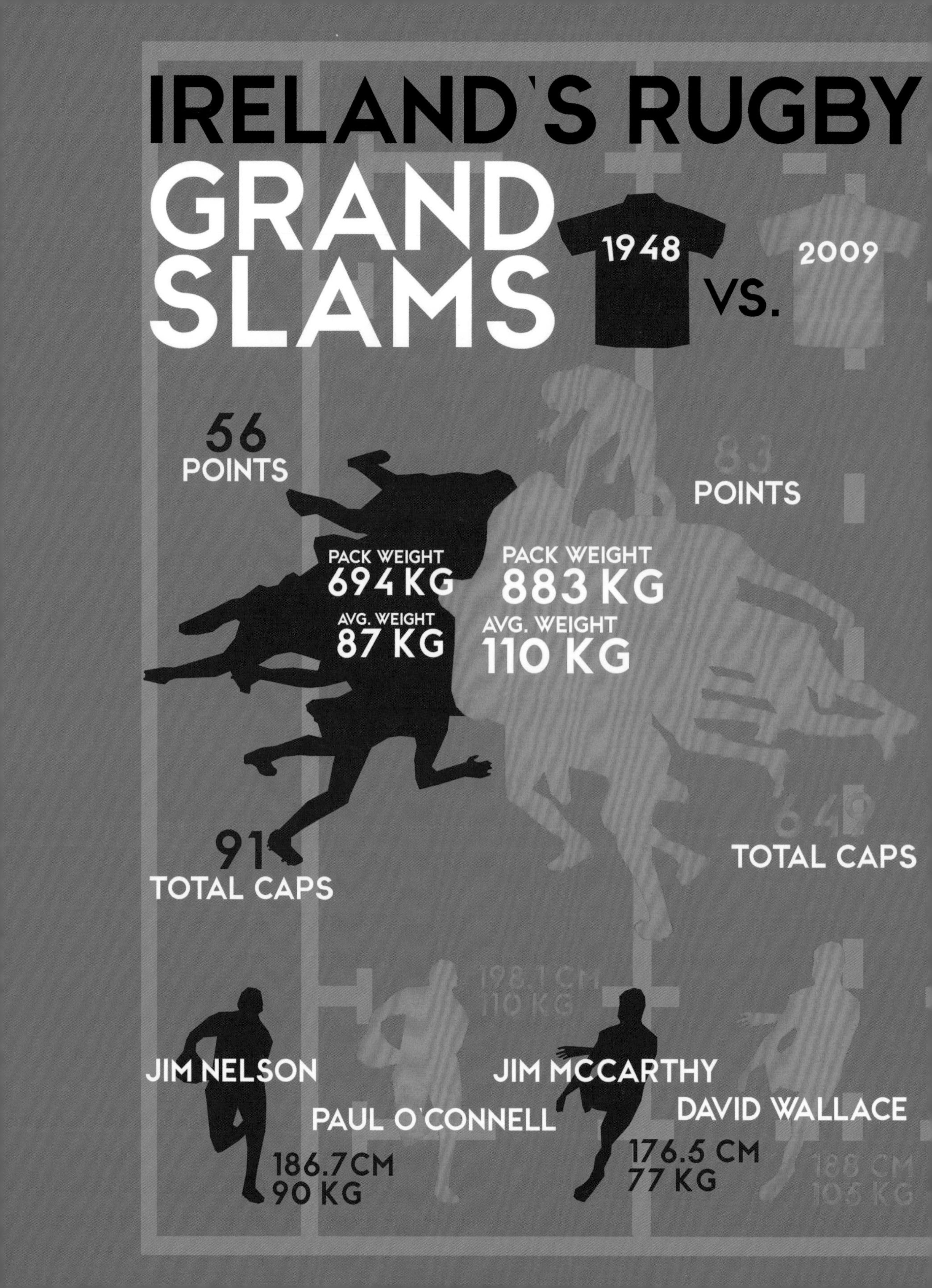

IRELAND'S RUGBY
GRAND SLAMS

1948 VS. 2009

56 POINTS

83 POINTS

PACK WEIGHT
694 KG

PACK WEIGHT
883 KG

AVG. WEIGHT
87 KG

AVG. WEIGHT
110 KG

91 TOTAL CAPS

64 TOTAL CAPS

198.1 CM
110 KG

JIM NELSON

JIM MCCARTHY

PAUL O'CONNELL

DAVID WALLACE

186.7 CM
90 KG

176.5 CM
77 KG

188 CM
105 KG

FRONT ROW

263 KG

338 KG

CONVERSION RATE

30%

86%

CONVERSIONS

DROP GOALS

NONE

PENALTIES

NONE

TRIES

Which Irish Grand Slam team was the best?

Break it down to the most basic psychology. Knock a man enough times and he will start to believe his own failures. The human spirit can only tolerate so much rejection before it begins to accept failure.

As Confucius said, 'Our greatest glory is not in never falling, it's in rising every time we fall.'

The Grand Slam-winning side of 2009 had suffered its fair share of failures before finally crossing the line in European rugby's premier tournament. The 'golden generation' had yet to win a single Six Nations title in almost a decade of trying when it embarked on its ground-breaking campaign that year. To say that Ireland had underachieved up until then is a massive understatement.

Eddie O'Sullivan had been extremely unlucky on a few occasions during his tenure in charge. The foot-and-mouth disaster of 2001 broke Ireland's momentum in what would otherwise have been a championship-winning campaign. Ireland's defeat to Scotland in a rearranged fixture in September ended any hopes of claiming the title. That defeat in Murrayfield was nothing short of disastrous. And it could not have come at a more crucial stage in the championship.

France broke Irish hearts in brutal fashion at Croke Park in 2007. With the game at Ireland's mercy, Vincent Clerc skipped through a vacant midfield to score a try under the posts and helped Ireland snatch defeat from the jaws of victory. It was a crushing blow for the coach and players alike. Ireland certainly did not deserve it.

When O'Sullivan stepped down after a disastrous 2007 World Cup campaign and a subsequent Six Nations fiasco in 2008, there was an air of disillusionment hanging heavily over the Irish team. The passionate optimism that had followed their fortunes religiously over the preceding years was beginning to waver and loyal fans openly questioned if their team would ever attain the holy grail.

It took a new coaching ticket to push Ireland over the line. Looking back on it now, it's difficult to suggest that Declan Kidney was solely responsible for Ireland's change in fortunes. Certainly, the former Munster coach had achieved his fair share of success with two Heineken Cup titles in 2006 and 2008, but to attribute that Grand Slam to Kidney alone would be to do O'Sullivan a great disservice.

There's no question that Ireland had underachieved during O'Sullivan's six-year tenure, but to dismiss his influence over that Grand Slam-winning team is ignorant in the extreme. For all of his flaws, O'Sullivan was an extremely gifted coach. The players, even those outside his circle of trust, will attest to that to this day. O'Sullivan laid the foundations and Kidney got Ireland over the line. It's as simple and as complicated as that.

That 2009 team stands apart. Their resilience as much as their talent got them there. Commentators and seasoned bar-stoolers will always remember Ronan O'Gara's magical drop goal in Cardiff but the reality is that the seeds of victory were sown in the many defeats and hardships suffered along the way. The victory over Wales was as much for the men who had sweated and slogged in the green jersey over previous campaigns as it was for the twenty-two squad members that memorable day.

Reggie Corrigan, Anthony Foley, Keith Wood, Keith Gleeson, David Humphreys, Denis

Hickie, Mick Galwey, Peter Clohessy, Eric Miller, Alan Quinlan – the list goes on and on. The Grand Slam was for every professional rugby player who had pulled on the green jersey over the previous ten years. It was a team effort. A squad effort. No man sailed alone.

We will remember these men. In years to come, when Leinster and Munster yearn for glories past and look back fondly on the days when European rugby bowed to the strength of Irish provinces, we will remember the Ireland team of 2009.

We will celebrate their bravery in never giving up. We will admire their resilience when championship titles escaped their grip, leaving them desolate and in despair. These Irish warriors refused to accept defeat, they kept coming and coming and coming.

Brian O'Driscoll's heroic try against England to seal victory. Jamie Heaslip's seventeen-stone side-stepping the French defence to touch down to a thunderous roar at Croke Park. Tommy Bowe pouncing on the beleaguered Welsh defence for an audacious try at the Millennium Stadium. And then there's ROG. That pass from his old school pal Stringer. The crowd numbed in anticipation and nerves. The focus … the strike … the elation. A moment frozen in rugby history. Then, in an instant, despair. Stephen Jones with a penalty opportunity to break Irish hearts once again. His eyes steeled to the Irish posts, the quiet hush in the Cardiff crowd. The strike, the heartbeat …

By the smallest margins we stand or fall. The margin, that day, was less than five feet. Ireland, so many times disappointed, had finally achieved their destiny. And it was just that. This team could not have left it any other way. A Grand Slam title was the least that they deserved – and, in 2009, it finally happened.

Team sport reduces grown men to vulnerable children. Rugby in particular requires complete trust in the man standing beside you. On his watch, you can crumple or soar. The Grand Slam-winning side of 2009 fought and died for each other several times over. They never admitted defeat in the face of bitter disappointments and they carried the ghosts of internationals past on their shoulders every step of the way. For that, they will always be remembered as sporting legends.

2009 TEAM:

Rob Kearney; Tommy Bowe, Brian O'Driscoll, Gordon D'Arcy, Luke Fitzgerald; Ronan O'Gara, Tomás O'Leary; Marcus Horan, Jerry Flannery, John Hayes; Donncha O'Callaghan, Paul O'Connell; Stephen Ferris, David Wallace, Jamie Heaslip

Subs: Rory Best, Tom Court, Mick O'Driscoll, Denis Leamy, Peter Stringer, Paddy Wallace, Geordan Murphy.

3 GREAT IRISH WINS AGAINST AUSTRALIA

1. 1958

Ireland's first win against one of the major southern hemisphere countries came at Lansdowne Road when they secured a famous victory 9–6.

The Irish selectors picked six new caps for the game, five of them in the pack. Three of the five forwards – Ronnie Dawson, Bill Mulcahy and Noel Murphy – would become Irish captains and Lions. Dawson and Murphy would also coach the Lions. The debutant in the three-quarter line was eighteen-year-old David Hewitt.

The Australians led for most of the game but Ireland snatched victory with a superb comeback which included two tries. Jack Kyle was magnificent against the wind as he coaxed his forwards up the touchline with accurate kicks, while using blindside breaks to link with wings Tony O'Reilly and Cecil Pedlow rather than risk a breakdown in midfield.

The fightback began with Gordon Wood charging down a kick and Dawson, on his debut, falling on the ball for a try to even the scores.

The youngster Hewitt had a nervous first half but covered himself in glory with an interception and pass to Noel Henderson which sent his burly partner on a forty-metre run to the line to claim a famous victory.

The match was also remembered for a notorious incident, when the Australian prop Nick Shehadie punched Murphy at the scrum. Interestingly, in his match report in *The Irish Times*, Paul McWeeney did not explicitly refer to the assault. A different era indeed.

Lungs aflame – Henderson makes the try line.

2.   1967

The summer of 1967 had one test scheduled, to be played at the Sydney Cricket Ground. Ireland travelled in reasonable confidence as the self-same opponents had been beaten the previous season at Lansdowne Road and, in the Five Nations Championship earlier in the year, Ireland had a reasonable campaign and though they had two surprising losses at Lansdowne Road, they had won both away games against Scotland and Wales.

Amongst the uncapped players in the tour party were two back-row forwards, Terry Moore of Highfield and Denis Hickie of St Mary's College. At the beginning of the tour, it seemed certain that the Mary's number eight would win his first cap. However, he was rested for the midweek game, and Moore had such an outstanding match that he won selection for the test match, to Hickie's intense disappointment.

What followed was a surprise to the small band of travelling Irish supporters and a monumental shock to Australian rugby. Ireland delivered victory by eleven points to five, which made them the first team from the northern hemisphere to win a game south of the equator against a major nation.

The Irish pack completely dominated their opponents, which nullified the threat of the outstanding Wallaby back division. In the week before the game, scrum-half Brendan Sherry was very doubtful but he was miraculously patched up by the team doctor, Jamsie Maher. It may have been the surgeon's finest hour, because in the second half, Sherry broke laterally from a ruck and dummied to out-half Mike Gibson, before passing the ball to centre Jerry Walsh who crashed over near the posts to give Tom Kiernan an easy conversion and seal a famous victory.

In a postscript to the game, four years later Ken Goodall made the surprising move to rugby league at Workington, and Ireland began the search for a new number eight to replace him. Hickie's career had been in the doldrums, but a late call-up for Leinster against Connacht was the precursor to an outstanding provincial campaign and selection for his first cap against France.

He was to win six caps for Ireland and the disappointment in Australia was erased.

3.   1979

I cannot do better than quote from Edmund Van Esbeck's report on this game in *The Irish Times*.

> 'Here on a foreign field, before a partisan and critical audience, Ireland gave a performance of record proportions, for never before in history has an Irish side

scored twenty-seven points in an international. Their victory margin of fifteen points was, too, the highest ever retained against Australia.'

He went on, '... not since the legendary Ned Kelly went on the rampage has any individual wreaked such damage on Australian soil as Campbell, cool and composed under pressure, brilliant in his application of tactics, and regal in his place and line kicking.'

Ollie Campbell's selection was a complete surprise as Tony Ward had gone on that tour as the man in possession of the number ten, and few imagined he would not be first choice for the position. It was indicative of the controversy that, almost fifty years later, discussions still rage amongst rugby aficionados as to which of the two was the better player.

Campbell's tally of four penalty goals, two conversions and one drop goal was a new points record for an Irish player in an international. To this day, the great fly-half, like Van Esbeck in his newspaper report, gives full credit to an outstanding performance by the pack.

In the championship, Ireland had used three full-backs and for the summer tour, the selectors had gambled on two uncapped players in the shape of Rodney O'Donnell and Frank Ennis. O'Donnell played in both test matches and was magnificent. He won four more caps and was selected for the Lions tour to South Africa where his career was tragically cut short by injury.

The 1979 tour of Australia remains one of the great achievements in Irish rugby history.

1991 RUGBY WORLD CUP

The 1991 World Cup was hosted by Wales with the other Five Nation countries hosting some games and, once again, I had a personal involvement. At the time, I was coach to Connacht and London Irish and Jim Staples, David Curtis and Simon Geoghegan had all played for me at Connacht and, of course, they played their club rugby at London Irish. Furthermore, Rob Saunders, the Ireland scrum-half, also played his rugby at Sunbury. So I was intimately involved in the playing careers of four of the Irish backline.

To add interest to the mix, Eddie O'Sullivan, who was my assistant at London Irish, was fitness adviser to Ciaran Fitzgerald, Ireland's coach for this World Cup. Incredibly, I also had a connection to Western Samoa, who were going to be the surprise of the tournament. Matt Keenan, the Samoan lock, had signed for London Irish and would be playing with the team after the World Cup ended.

Rugby in the United States was at a low ebb and the team arrived in London with little or no hope of improving on the performance of 1987. As expected, they lost all three games in the group stages to New Zealand, England and Italy.

Italy delivered a warning that was not heeded by the nations of the home championship. In attempting to strengthen Italian domestic rugby, the authorities had recruited a great number of foreign players. The problem was that this created a massive shortage of players in key positions who were qualified to play for Italy. Twenty years later, the major countries of Europe are facing a similar problem, as foreign players litter the team sheets of clubs.

There were two big surprises in the pool stages. Canada beat Fiji to reach the knockout stages of the competition for the first and only time in their history. However, the biggest surprise of all was when Western Samoa knocked Wales out of contention in front of a home crowd in Cardiff. The Islanders were a disparate group, having selected many Samoan-qualified players who were playing in New Zealand, but they were welded into a team and made a mockery of the decision to omit them from the tournament four years earlier.

The quarter-finals went according to plan, with the possible exception of lower ranked England beating France at Parc des Princes. But it was Lansdowne Road that witnessed two of the great matches of the tournament. The quarter-final between Australia and Ireland was a titanic struggle and when Gordon Hamilton went over for a try in the corner after a move that had gone seventy-five metres, it seemed that Ireland had delivered a

They think it's all over – but it isn't.

monumental upset. Sadly it was not to be, as Rob Saunders missed touch from the restart and David Campese scored a try in the corner to destroy Ireland's hopes.

So Ireland's interest in the competition ended at the quarter-final stage, and we still await the day that green shirts will be seen in the penultimate stage of the Rugby World Cup.

Having beaten Ireland, Australia faced New Zealand in the semi-final at Lansdowne Road. The Wallabies, in a masterpiece of public relations, checked in to a city-centre hotel and in the week of the game could be seen on Dublin's streets in their distinctive tracksuits, happily signing autographs and posing for pictures.

In contrast, the Kiwis, as was their wont, retreated to a camp in the countryside and kept very much to themselves. The result was that the neutrals in the crowd at Lansdowne Road were behind Australia and were delighted when the pre-tournament favourites were knocked out.

Interestingly for what most rugby followers would have seen as a must-see match, tickets were easily available. I can remember standing on a chair in the foyer of the Berkeley Court Hotel, holding up two premium-stand tickets for the match and there were no takers even though I was giving them away for nothing.

In the final at Twickenham, England were beaten by Australia and, yet again, there were many empty seats in the stadium. The Rugby World Cup had yet to capture the imagination.

The club game

It was a cold, wet Sunday afternoon at Dr Hickey Park, when the J3's from Greystones and St Mary's took to the pitch. The small crowd huddling together in the stand roared their appreciation as Greystones' tight-head Willie Byrne and Mary's loose-head Sammy Brennan approached each other on the halfway line to shake hands.

'Good luck, old pal,' Willie grinned, his arm outstretched.

'I don't need it, as you well know,' Sammy replied.

They turned, smiling, and headed back to their team-mates, readying themselves for battle. Over the next eighty minutes, Willie and Sammy pushed, pulled, wrestled and scrapped with each other until the match was over. Both sucked in the air, exhausted and sore from their efforts. When the final whistle sounded, they made their way towards the halfway line once more. Bloodied but smiling, they shook hands and side by side marched off the pitch to the club bar for a well-deserved pint. Willie is forty-two years of age and Sammy is ten years his senior.

What motivates those two men to keep going in the most physically demanding of sports well into their forties and fifties? Is it love for the game? Possibly. But there is more to it than that. Rugby union in Ireland has its history and its roots in the hundreds of clubs around the country. The elite group of players at the highest level do not proportionately reflect the work and effort that goes into sustaining rugby at grass-roots level. Brian O'Driscoll, Ronan O'Gara and Paul O'Connell all began their careers with their clubs. Today, thousands of coaches, parents, volunteers and committee members work tirelessly for little or no reward, other than to see their clubs prosper and thrive. Without them, the game would collapse. Kids would

Willie Byrne of Greystones and Sammy Brennan of St Mary's face each other in a club match at Donnybrook. Their mutual respect was born from a fierce club rivalry.

have nowhere to go on Sunday mornings and thousands of young rugby players would be lost to other sports. Without the clubs, rugby in Ireland would cease to exist.

However, since the professional game has taken off, club rugby in Ireland has been tossed onto the scrapheap. The lifeblood of the game in Ireland, where young kids learn their trade and where men and women go to play and socialise, has been cast aside in favour of the

The champion club deserved better than this.

new kid in town – Leinster, Munster, Ulster and Connacht extract every drop of coverage in the media and attract all sorts of punters through the gates on match day. There is no room left for the clubs. Scheduling conflicts with the professional game have resulted in supporter numbers dropping at league and cup matches across the board. Revenue has dried up and many clubs are now battling for survival.

Over the past seven or eight years, fans have been spoiled for choice. On any given weekend during the season, it is possible to switch on the television and watch five or six live games over the course of seventy-two hours. Often, these high-profile, professional games in the European Cup or domestic league are taking place at the same time as AIL games are kicking off across the country. The provinces, to their credit, do their best to stagger kick-off times throughout the season, so as not to clash with AIL matches, but the reality is that, because of time and financial constraints, many fans are unlikely to attend two live games in the one day. It's the clubs that inevitably suffer. Supporting the local club has become a lot less appealing and a lot more difficult.

The IRFU are not helping matters. Take the 2013 Bateman Cup as an example. After a long, hard season battling through their provincial section and an All-Ireland semi-final, Cork Constitution of Munster and St Mary's of Leinster were relishing the prospect of a cup final clash. Both teams had under-performed in the league campaign but were excited at the idea of ending the season with some silverware. The decision was made to toss a coin to decide the venue, with St Mary's winning out and opting for Templeville Road in Dublin. In their infinite wisdom, the IRFU schedule the match on the same day as Munster's Heineken Cup semi-final against Clermont Auvergne in Montpellier and Leinster's Amlin Challenge Cup semi-final against Biarritz at the RDS.

So, instead of having the cup final as a stand-alone fixture when a decent crowd could be expected to turn out and support both teams, they shoved it into an already congested Saturday afternoon when Leinster and Munster were competing in European action. To suggest it was farcical and disrespectful to all involved is an understatement. As it happened, Mary's and Con kicked off at noon that Saturday in front of about 150 people. The atmosphere was poor because of the small crowd, but the players got on with the job and played out an entertaining and high-scoring game at the end of which Cork Con had withstood a late Mary's fightback to win the cup for the third time. The television cameras picked up the delighted faces of the winning squad celebrating their victory, but the whole occasion was extremely shabbily treated.

I remember attending a match in Greystones in the early 1990s and thinking nothing of seeing two trainloads of Young Munster supporters walking from the station to the rugby club. A few weeks later, the television cameras were down at Dr Hickey Park and several thousand people were present to see Greystones play St Mary's where there were a number of internationals and even Lions on show. After the match, a few stragglers came into the clubhouse to join in the post-match celebrations, and attested to hearing, from the other side of town, the cheers from the crowd every time Greystones scored that afternoon. Those days are long gone now.

Fans and regular attenders of the professional game blame a poor standard of play for keeping them away from club matches. It is an accusation that League of Ireland soccer also has to contend with on a regular basis. In truth, the current standard of AIL is probably not a million miles away from the glory days of the league. But, again, viewers are so spoiled for choice these days with professional rugby available every weekend on television that comparing like with like probably isn't very fair.

The simple fact is that the clubs competing in the AIL can't get regular access to their top players. The IRFU's diktat that only two senior contracted provincial players per club can line out every week prohibits many fringe professionals from participating in the league, even when they are available. I refuse to believe that the best way of bringing younger players through is to prevent them from playing for their clubs in the AIL.

Take a young player just out of school at Pres Cork. A place in the Munster academy beckons and he duly commits to the underage system with the province. Training routines and matches against fellow academy players become the norm while he works away at improving his game with the best of facilities on offer. He progresses to a development contract after three years and continues to compete against guys in the same environment, sporadically turning out for his club. He serves his time on a development contract, making a handful of senior appearances in the process before being promoted to a full senior contract. He is now twenty-four years of age and has spent the majority of his career thus far scrummaging and competing against guys in a similar position. All of a sudden, he is thrown into a Pro12 match or a Heineken Cup game, and is expected to go up against grizzled opponents, eight years his senior. He gets eaten alive, chewed up and spat out – and wonders why he cannot compete.

The guys who are training with the academies or on development contracts with the provinces are effectively full-time professional athletes. They eat, sleep and train as senior contracted players, so the gap in standard between them and players of similar age who hold down full-time jobs outside of rugby and who might train only twice a week is growing with every season. Unless the IRFU change their attitude and approach to the club game, it won't be long before we arrive at a stage where contracted players won't be allowed to compete in the amateur leagues at all, for health and safety reasons.

Financially, many rugby clubs are in crisis. The decline in supporter numbers coupled with the depreciation of traditional sources of sponsorship has meant revenues are at an all-time low. Many clubs have shredded their budgets but, for some, it is still not enough. Committees spend a lot of their time looking at alternative ways of bringing in revenue, with a lot of clubs hiring out their facilities for social functions and parties. Some don't even have that option. Membership fees and revenue from social functions rarely come close to covering the cost of running a club and with sponsorship and advertising still in decline, clubs are relying on members and outside help to keep themselves afloat.

The IRFU have a duty to step in and do something about this. It doesn't take a genius to figure out that if the clubs could get more support from the governing body, and from the provinces themselves, there could be a system in place that benefited everybody in the game. It's not difficult to see that the clubs competing in the top tier of the domestic league can be of great benefit to the provinces, and vice versa. If a proper structure is put in place, with rules and guidelines on player use and co-operation from all sides, the AIL can be revived. It may never get back to the glory days of the amateur game, but it must have a role in the future of the game in this country.

Fixing the club game

Below is my suggestion to solve the current problems facing the AIL. It's not perfect, but it's a start.

A new sixteen-team All-Ireland League Division 1 is set up.

After inviting applicants to compete in the league, the IRFU designates four clubs in each of the provinces as Tier One Clubs, based on a number of different criteria, and places them into a feeder system with the four professional provinces.

For example:
- **Leinster:** Lansdowne, Clontarf, St Mary's, Blackrock College
- **Munster:** Cork Con, Garryowen, Shannon, Young Munster
- **Ulster:** Ballymema, Queen's University, Dungannon, Belfast Harlequins
- **Connacht:** Galwegians, Corinthians, Sligo, Ballinasloe.

Each of the sixteen clubs develops training programmes and player schedules in conjunction with the provinces, while competing in the new AIL Division 1. Each year, the top four clubs at the end of the season compete in a semi-final play-off and a final to decide the eventual league champions. The bottom club in the table is relegated to Division 2, with the top side in Division 2 being promoted to Division 1.

At the end of the season, the clubs in Division 1 compete in a draft system for the next batch of players coming through the provincial academies. Picks are awarded on the basis of the previous season's league table position with the bottom team allowed first pick and so on up the ranks. The newly promoted side from Division 2 gets the first three picks on the draft.

Academy, development and senior contracted players who are not involved with the provinces on match weekends are released to play for their clubs in the AIL. There are no restrictions on the number of senior contracted players who can line out each week, as long as the province has given them the all clear.

Training schedules between province and club allow academy and development players to train with their clubs for a minimum of two nights per week.

The rest of the clubs in Ireland are assigned to Divisions 2, 3 and 4 (based on criteria) with a play-off and promotion–relegation system in place.

Each season, an All-Ireland Cup is held with clubs from all divisions involved in an open-draw, knockout competition.

The club game in Ireland grows steadily as work with the provinces means the standard increases across the board. Crowds and gate receipts also increase with fans coming to see the next generation of stars and players on the fringes of the professional setup lining out

for their club. A league sponsor is sought and a television rights deal is offered to interested broadcasters. The finances are split amongst the participating clubs, with prize money for the league and cup also assigned.

Clubs in the lower divisions are also supported through a system of grants and bonuses, and the incentive for all lower division sides is to make it through to Division 1.

As I said, the above idea is not without problems, but I believe it has a lot of merit and should be considered. The club game in Ireland is worth saving. There is too much history and passion rooted in the domestic setup to not at least try and revive it. Drive down to Temple Hill on a Sunday morning and try telling the 500 kids in Cork Con gear that their club means nothing in the greater scheme of things. Or try telling Sammy Brennan at St Mary's that his five decades in a blue jersey were all in vain. The heart of the club game still beats loudly in Irish rugby circles but it desperately needs help or it could die off altogether. And that would be unforgivable and tragic in the extreme.

Opposite page: The under-19 development squads from Ireland and England play a friendly at Old Belvedere.

Leinster V Munster

Leinster v. Munster is Irish rugby's greatest rivalry. And, negative associations aside, the battle between these two provinces has been hugely beneficial for the Irish game. The success of Munster in the Heineken Cup in 2006 and 2008 forced Leinster to up the ante and chase the high standard that had been set by their neighbour. It was Munster that broke the mould in Europe and without that victory over Biarritz in Cardiff in 2006, Leinster might never have gone on to claim the trophy on three subsequent occasions. Munster set the standard, Leinster duly followed – and Irish rugby was the overall winner.

The rivalry exploded into life on 4 April 2006 when both sides clashed in the semi-final of the Heineken Cup. The nation was consumed by rugby in the build-up to the game with every dog on the street speculating about who would come out on top. It was billed as the clash of the Leinster backs and the Munster forwards and two styles of rugby that were poles apart. Leinster had scored thirty-two tries in the seven rounds leading up to the semi-final and were seen as slight favourites after an incredible performance against Toulouse in the quarter-final.

The scrap for tickets in the week leading up to the game was frenzied. Everyone wanted to be at Lansdowne Road to witness what many felt would be a landmark game in Irish rugby. But when the teams walked out of the tunnel and onto the pitch that afternoon, it was immediately apparent that Munster had won the first battle. The stadium was a magnificent cauldron of Munster red. It must have been a shock to the Leinster squad. After all, this was Lansdowne Road – Leinster's home, in the middle of Dublin. Munster invaders had taken over the heart of Leinster rugby and it was an incredible sight to behold.

If Munster fans drew first blood by their presence alone, it didn't take long for their team to follow suit. Munster attacked their Irish rivals like a pack of ravenous dogs, snapping at Leinster heels and never giving their opponents an inch. Paul O'Connell was immense, tearing into tackles in the loose and setting the platform for victory with his leadership and aggression. Denis Leamy burst over for the first of Munster's three tries early in the first half and Leinster simply had no answers to give. They were blitzed and shell-shocked. Ronan

O'Gara epitomised the ice-cool general for Munster, directing his troops around the pitch with confidence and control while simultaneously holding Leinster's backline at bay.

Denis Leamy, David Wallace and Anthony Foley hounded Leinster's fly-half Felipe Contepomi until the Argentina international eventually cracked under the pressure and lost his temper, resulting in a Munster penalty. O'Gara duly obliged and added three points with his boot. The Munster masterplan was in full effect. When O'Gara danced his way through the Leinster defence to score Munster's second try, the result was beyond doubt. Trevor Halstead's late intercept from a Guy Easterby pass was just the icing on the cake. Munster were through to their third Heineken Cup final in six years and nothing, it seemed, was going to deny them the title.

That semi-final victory set down a marker in Irish rugby. Leinster coach Michael Cheika received a fair bit of criticism in post-match analysis for the way his side approached the game. Many felt Leinster weren't mentally up to the challenge and the fault was laid at the Australian's feet. It was suggested that Cheika's lack of understanding of the rivalry between the provinces contributed to Leinster's flat performance. That may have been partly true, but to focus on that would be to do Munster a huge disservice. Leinster were completely outplayed on their home patch by a stronger, hungrier team. That defeat left a bitter taste in

all Leinster mouths, but it would be three more years before they would get the opportunity for revenge.

The build-up to the Heineken Cup semi-final in 2009 had all the intensity and anticipation of its predecessor. Munster were aiming for their third title triumph, having beaten Toulouse in the 2008 final, while Leinster continued to search for their own holy grail, having played second fiddle to their near neighbours for the best part of half a decade.

Cheika's side needed little motivation as the showdown in front of 82,000 spectators loomed. Leinster's itch was far greater and their hunger and desperation shone through from the very first minute at Croke Park. The game was a particularly poignant one for Jonathan Sexton, who was sprung from the bench midway through the first half. An injury to Felipe Contepomi catapulted Sexton into the spotlight and the young fly-half grabbed his opportunity with both hands. His first touch of the ball resulted in three points for Leinster, as he held his nerve to slot a difficult penalty and push his side 6–3 in front. When Gordon D'Arcy burrowed his way over the line for the game's first try, Leinster were firmly in control, though they only led by five points at the break, 11–6.

Munster's task was made all the more difficult in the second half when Luke Fitzgerald took a pass from Shane Horgan to beat the defence and touch down. Now Leinster had their breathing space and could afford to ease off, but they weren't finished yet. In beautiful symmetry to Halstead's try three years earlier, Brian O'Driscoll intercepted the ball to sprint clear and secure a Leinster win. His man of the match performance inspired Leinster to a hugely important victory and any question marks that had lingered over their mental strength before kick-off were well and truly put to bed. Munster's crown had been wrestled from them and the 25–6 scoreline did not flatter the victors in the least. Like Munster in 2006, Leinster went on to win the Heineken Cup that year and with it their first European trophy.

There is little doubt that Munster's successes in 2006 and 2008 stirred something deep within the Leinster camp. That they rose to the challenge and even surpassed Munster's haul with a third Heineken Cup triumph in 2012 speaks volumes for how far Leinster came in such a short period of time. Munster will stop at nothing to make sure the recent run of results between the sides is reversed. I certainly wouldn't bet against it happening soon.

The passionate rivalry between the provinces continues today. The Heineken Cup battles of 2006 and 2009 have been interspersed with numerous encounters in the Pro12; each one as intense and exciting as the one that preceded it. I can honestly say that I have yet to witness a dull meeting between the sides. As long as we have rugby in Ireland, we will have Leinster v. Munster.

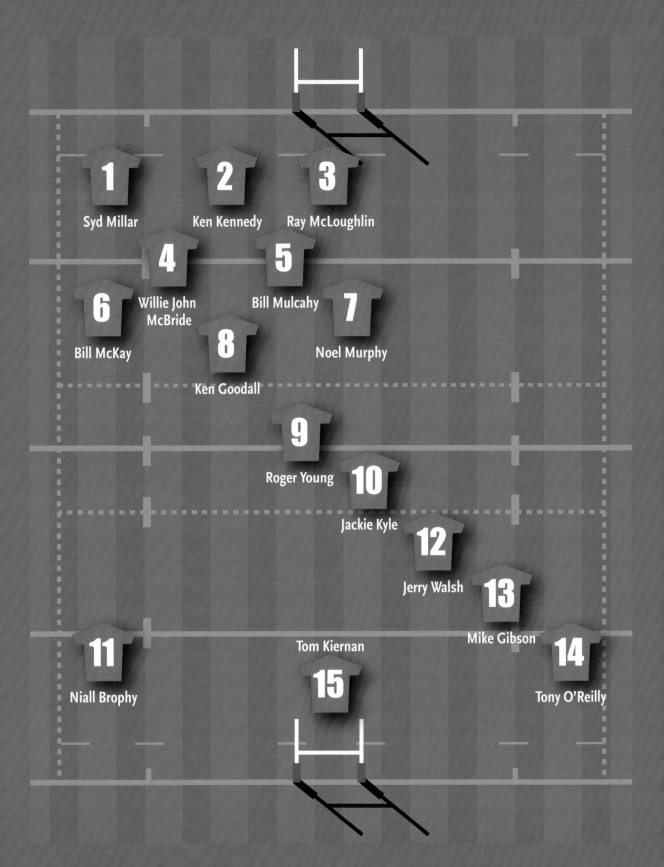

MY GREATEST IRISH TEAM
1948–1973

 15 Tom Kiernan

A certainty for selection and, in this particular team, also has the captaincy. Kiernan was magnificent under the high ball with outstanding positional sense. He was also a great innovator as he had to adjust his game when the principle of the attacking full-back was developed. He also excited crowds at Lansdowne Road as he found new ways of using the ball when kicking to touch was restricted outside the twenty-two.

Honourable mentions: George Norton and Paddy Berkery

 14 Tony O'Reilly

His greatness is determined by his performance in two Lions tours. He went to South Africa as a teenager and created a try-scoring record. Four years later, he was back in New Zealand and created another record. He was unfortunate to play in the centre for Ireland, which was never his best position, as he flourished when playing outside good passers. Tall, strong and good looking, he was the first superstar of rugby.

Honourable mentions: Mick Lane, Pat Casey and Alan Duggan

Mike Gibson

Gibson would easily challenge Brian O'Driscoll as Ireland's best centre of all time. He was hugely influential on the Lions tour of 1971 but, above all, he raised the standards for all his contemporaries. It is very hard to find a weakness in his game.

Honourable mentions: Dave Hewitt and Kevin Flynn

Jerry Walsh

This may be a surprising choice but, at inside-centre, Walsh was probably the best defender Ireland has ever seen. His tackling was of such a destructive nature that it became an attacking tool. He was hugely underrated as an attacker and tragically his Lions tour in 1966 was cut short by the death of his father when he had to return home.

Honourable mentions: Noel Henderson

Niall Brophy

Tall but with the pace of a 200-metre runner, Brophy fully earned selection on two Lions tours. He was a potent attacker and a very clever defender – to this day, his views on defence out wide merit attention. He was cruelly struck down by injury in Australia on the 1959 Lions tour and had to return home; however, an early injury in South Africa in 1964 did not have the same catastrophic effect and Brophy fought back to gain a test place.

Honourable mentions: Bertie O'Hanlon, Cecil Pedlow and Maurice Mortell

Jackie Kyle

Like Tom Kiernan at full-back, Kyle bestrides his position like a colossus. Simply no contest.

Honourable mentions: Mick English and Barry McGann

9 Roger Young

When a player goes from Queen's University second fifteen to the Irish team, he has to be something special. Young was such a player who was selected by Ulster when he was unable to gain a place on the university team. It turned out to be a prescient selection, and he went on to be selected for two Lions tours, a testament to his strengths behind beaten packs and his strong kicking game.

Honourable mentions: John O'Meara, Andy Mulligan and John Maloney

8 Ken Goodall

Had he not gone to rugby league because of the financial pressures of marriage, Ken Goodall might well have become the best number eight the game has ever seen, and Mervyn Davies might have been a footnote in rugby history. Goodall was tall, rangy and hugely skilful.

Honourable mentions: Des O'Brien, Ronnie Kavanagh and Ron Lamont

7 Noel Murphy

A selection sure to cause much discussion in Cork as Kyle's 'dispatch rider' does not make the cut. Murphy started as an open-side forward, before becoming a powerful presence on the other flank. He was selected for two Lions tours and would certainly have made it a third had he not broken his collarbone against England at Twickenham. He beats McCarthy on the grounds of greater physical presence and his test match selections for the Lions.

Honourable mentions: Jim McCarthy and Mick Doyle

Bill McKay

Another certainty. This veteran of the Second World War was a powerhouse blindside flanker for Ireland and the Lions. At one point in the 1950 tour to New Zealand, McKay had scored six tries in seven appearances. Such was his importance to the side that, after breaking his nose in the second test and missing a number of games, he was picked for the third test wearing a face mask. He was powerful in the tight, a tremendous ball carrier and one of the few home-based players to impress the Kiwis.

Honourable mentions: Mick Hipwell and Stewart McKinney

Bill Mulcahy

This team has two front-of-the-line jumpers, although in the era they operated, it would hardly have made much difference. They also played together for Ireland, so no doubt sorted it out. Mulcahy liked the ball thrown 'hard, low and crooked' at the lineout, which was the methodology of the time. He was good enough to make two Lions tours and hold down a test place at wing-forward.

Honourable mentions: Gerry Culliton and Mick Molloy

Willie John McBride

Hardly any room for discussion about a forward who was capped sixty-three times for Ireland and earned seventeen test caps on five Lions tours. McBride competed toe to toe with some of the best lock forwards in the world. The lineout was hardly his strong point but, in an era when the set piece was 'the illegitimate child of rugby football', as Ray McLoughlin christened it, Willie John was a bruiser at the front giving his opponents little space.

Honourable mentions: Jimmie Nelson and Tom Reid

3 Ray McLoughlin

McLoughlin started his career as a destructive tight-head scrummager. His first five opponents in international rugby lost their place after playing against him. After injury had ruled him out for a number of seasons, he saw an opportunity to revive his international career as a loose-head prop. Not only did he succeed in that aspiration, but he went on another Lions tour, although he was unlucky enough to be injured early on. He is probably the greatest technician of all time in the position.

Honourable mentions: Gordon Wood and Sean Lynch

2 Ken Kennedy

Kennedy beats iconic performers like Karl Mullen and Ronnie Dawson for the number two shirt because the Ulsterman set new standards of fitness and technique. He was ahead of his time and very much in the mould of the modern hooker, who is an ancillary flanker. He twice toured with the Lions, in 1966 and 1974.

Honourable mentions: Karl Mullen and Ronnie Dawson

1 Syd Millar

Like McLoughlin, Millar could play with equal facility on either side of the scrum. He made an astonishing forty-three appearances for the Lions over three tours and appeared in test matches against Australia, South Africa and New Zealand. Also like McLoughlin, he returned to the Irish team after an absence of five seasons. For longevity, technique and Lions performance, he is a must selection.

Honourable mentions: J.C. Daly, Tom Clifford and P.J. O'Donoghue

3 GREAT TOURNAMENTS

1. Six Nations Championship

I never feel the depression and gloom that most people experience in the immediate aftermath of the Christmas holidays. As the food and drink from weeks of overindulgence begins to leave the system, my focus turns to the start of the RBS Six Nations Championship. When others are busy batting away the January blues by forking out too much money for the gym or frantically trying to zip up their favourite pair of skinny jeans that now refuse to go past their knees, I'm preparing for seven weeks of international rugby.

The anticipation that comes with the opening weekend of the Six Nations never fails to excite me – six international teams, six blank canvasses and the promise of seven weeks of thrills, spills and rugby mania. What's not to love? Over the years, I have experienced every possible emotion watching Ireland compete for the championship title. I have been left gob-smacked by wonderful performances that I never saw coming, dismayed by disasters I could never have predicted and flattened by some of the most fascinating rugby I've ever had the pleasure of watching. French flair, Scottish stubbornness, English muscle, Welsh wizardry, Italian lunacy. I've seen it all and I've loved every single minute.

Each country brings their own unique ingredient to the melting pot. England over the years have done little to address their reputation as a big, hard-hitting side that relishes the physical confrontation up front. The RFU would like to think that they have produced some wonderfully talented backs over the years, but England's style of play is reliant on the Martin Johnsons, the Lawrence Dallaglios and the Neil Backs to snuff out the opposition and beat them to a pulp. It's a strategy that has garnered them some success over the years, but it has also left them very limited in their approach.

The French are the aristocrats of the European game. They pride themselves on their ability to strike from anywhere, and I firmly believe France would rather lose playing magnificent rugby than follow England's boring route to victory. French rugby is based on soft hands, quick feet and a swagger that would not be out of place on a catwalk in Paris. The French bring so much to the championship.

Wales have rediscovered their form over the past four years, against all manner of obstacles. Despite huge problems at club level, the Welsh have managed to produce a crop of strong, fit warriors who are capable of beating any team on their day. Wales supporters had to endure a pretty dour few years when the Six Nations succeeded the old Five Nations tournament. Ireland regularly toppled the once-proud rugby country both home and away, and it looked for a while like Wales' once-great reputation would disappear forever. The resurgence is difficult to explain if you consider the performance of the professional regions in European competition. The Ospreys have been the most successful side with a couple of league titles to their name, but, aside from that, Welsh clubs have struggled to compete in the Heineken Cup. The financial limits for players' wages have seen many of the big-name international stars leave Wales for clubs in France and England. So far, it doesn't seem to have had much impact on the national side, but I wonder what the future holds for rugby in Wales.

The future for Scotland is also unclear. Glasgow Warriors led a mini-revival in the 2012–2013 Pro12 season under their impressive head coach, former Scotland fly-half, Gregor Townsend. But is it a sign of future success in the region or the beginning of another false dawn? Edinburgh, meanwhile, had a disastrous year, culminating in their worst ever Pro12 finish and a Heineken Cup campaign without a single victory. Michael Bradley has paid for it with his job. Scotland continue to struggle with Italy for the wooden spoon in the Six Nations and, though there is the making of a good squad there, it remains to be seen if they can turn talent into results.

The old Five Nations Championship sustained European rugby fans for the best part of sixty years. During that time, Ireland managed to win seven championship titles, with England and France dominating the majority of the rest, excluding Wales' incredible side in the 1970s. But with the introduction of professional rugby towards the end of the 1990s, many at the top level felt a change of structure was needed. Professional rugby demanded bigger exposure and the feeling was that if the IRB were to sustain a professional game, they would have to increase their promotion of rugby union outside of the top five European countries.

The addition of Italy to the northern hemisphere's premier international rugby competition sparked new life into the tournament. The Italians, like Argentina, had been looking desperately for a tournament home, but it was 2000 before they were finally allowed to join England, Ireland, France, Scotland and Wales in a new-look Six Nations Championship. For me, the decision to admit Italy was an easy one. In order for the Azzurri to develop as a rugby-playing nation, they needed to compete regularly in top-flight competition. The new Six Nations tournament gave them an opportunity to do just that.

Cometh the hour, cometh the man – Ronan O'Gara drops the winning goal.

Life in the Six Nations Championship was always going to be difficult for Italy. In their first tournament, they finished bottom of the table and were without a win. Interestingly though, they managed to score nine tries that year, the same number as Scotland and one more than Wales. Their style of rugby was brash, direct and hugely reliant on their brute physical strength. They fell down technically and their fitness levels across the board were way off the other five teams. But since then, and despite nine wooden spoons from fourteen championships, they have steadily improved. Their fitness levels have increased dramatically and they have developed into a very difficult side to beat. Gone are the days when the other five countries could expect to put forty or fifty points on the Azzurri. Two victories in the past three years against France tells us everything we need to know about how far Italy have progressed. At this rate, it won't be long before we have six teams competing, each capable of winning the championship outright.

As for my favourite memories over the past thirteen years? There have been so many, but Ireland's Grand Slam decider against Wales stands out. If I could sum up Ronan O'Gara's incredible career in five seconds of action, it would be his match-winning drop goal at the Millennium Stadium. How many times has the Munster man dragged Ireland to victory against the odds over the years? That stage, in March 2009, was built for O'Gara.

There was never any doubt in my mind that he would take charge at that moment and strike for victory. The few tense minutes after that drop goal, when Stephen Jones' penalty kick fell just short of the crossbar, played havoc with every Irish fan's nerves, but I never doubted Ireland would come out on top. It was our day. And it was just reward for every player who had pulled on the green jersey in that momentous campaign.

For another incredible memory, what about Shane Horgan's try in Croke Park against England in 2007? The beautiful cross-field kick from O'Gara, the outstretched arms of Horgan reaching for the skies and the touchdown to thunderous applause and excitement from the delirious crowd. It was a moment fitting for the occasion. English players, on GAA turf, being taught a lesson in passion, commitment and skill.

The Six Nations Championship has also coincided with the explosion of a golden generation of Irish players – Brian O'Driscoll, Paul O'Connell, Gordon D'Arcy, David Wallace, Stephen Ferris, Ronan O'Gara, Peter Stringer ... these men set the standard for others with their dedication in training and professionalism on and off the pitch. That they all came through to play for Ireland at the same time was brilliant for Irish rugby. They will be hugely missed when they eventually decide to call it a day, and I wonder if we will ever have such a talented group available for Irish selection again.

The Six Nations Championship continues to delight and surprise millions of fans across Europe, but there is room for improvement. The sooner a bonus-point system is brought in, the better for everyone. There needs to be an incentive for teams to push on and score tries, even when the game is already won. The 2013 championship produced one of the most exciting first rounds in many years, but the tournament badly needs a fresh injection of ideas to sustain its appeal. The Heineken Cup has become a real rival to the international competition and unless the Six Nations committee moves with the times, they could find themselves left behind. I've no doubt change will happen, but why wait?

As for Ireland – a new era approaches with Joe Schmidt taking over the job of head coach from Declan Kidney. Schmidt's record with Leinster suggests that he is the perfect man to develop some of the younger players coming through and to bring Ireland to the next level. Best of all, he bases his rugby philosophy around perfecting the finer arts of the game. He is a coach who believes that the best way to break down opposition sides is to pass the ball.

I have high hopes for the future with Schmidt in charge, I just hope he will be allowed to do his job without outside interference. It's about time Ireland got another Six Nations title in the bag.

2. Bermuda Classic

The North Atlantic Ocean that surrounds the island of Bermuda is a fickle friend to its 64,000 inhabitants. On a calm autumn day, her light, blue waves lap the sandy shores of her beaches like horses' tongues on a morning canter but whenever the strong winds blow, the ocean responds with ravaging and mesmerising consequences. Any week, the shores of Bermuda experience every inch of both ends of the spectrum – glorious swimming conditions in a relaxed warm sea on a Saturday and currents and waves like something out of a tropical storm twenty-four hours later.

Such is this island's vulnerable position off the east coast of the United States that her living conditions are dominated completely by the fancy of the elements. A hot summer's day can be stifled and ruined by an overbearing humidity, while a winter's stroll on the beach is regularly whipped up into a hurricane in a matter of seconds. Where the weather is concerned, the only constant presence on this wonderful island is the promise of inconsistency.

Island mentality is something Irish people know plenty about, but I believe it is the Bermudians who encapsulate perfectly what this term is all about. Everything in Bermuda moves at an easier pace, from the cars and scooters travelling at the thirty miles an hour speed limit along the narrow, winding roads to the waiters and waitresses serving food and drinks in the many wonderful bars and restaurants across the country.

Nobody rushes in Bermuda because nobody has to hurry. It's not so much a mindset as a way of life. Thirty minutes to receive a main course in a restaurant enables the indulgence of another glass of wine. Getting stuck in rush-hour traffic just means more time to listen to the music on the radio. Car horns sound from morning till midnight in a friendly greeting to passers-by and familiar faces. People smile a lot too, and it becomes infectious.

I travel to Bermuda as often as my work schedule permits to attend the World Rugby Classic. This annual event at the National Sports Centre, just outside the capital Hamilton invites former rugby greats to come and participate in an eight-nation tournament over the course of seven glorious days. Every year, the British and Irish Classic Lions, coached by the wonderful and legendary Willie John McBride, are joined by the likes of South Africa, Australia, New Zealand, Italy, Argentina, France, the USA and Canada and a feast of social rugby takes place over the course of the week. The main requirement set down by John Kane, the President of the World Rugby Classic, is that each team consists only of retired players who have ended their full-time or professional careers. The tournament committee sets a minimum age of thirty-three (though exceptions can be made).

The Classic has hosted many great rugby names over the years. Jeremy Guscott and Francois Pienaar both attest to having a wonderful time, both on and off the field, during

Two of the greatest Lions – Willie John and JPR.

their trips. Both Classics have boasted a wealth of international experience in recent years, with the likes of Malcolm O'Kelly, Shane Byrne, David Corkery, Girvan Dempsey, Brian O'Meara, James Topping and Mark Blair representing Ireland, while the Bermuda locals have watched star names like Percy Montgomerie, Justin Marshall, A.J. Venter, Josh Lewsey, Tony Marsh, Robbie Fleck, Jeremy Paul and Colin Charvis line out for their respective teams.

John Kane, an Irishman originally from County Dublin, has been living in Bermuda for over forty years and he is the sole reason why this tournament has continued to thrive and prosper every year since its inception back in 1988. His love of rugby union, coupled with an unyielding faith in the benefits that go with hosting the World Rugby Classic, has meant that this week-long event has become a steadfast and eagerly anticipated tradition in the calendar of the local people. In fact, without help from the hundreds of local volunteers, it's safe to suggest the tournament simply would not happen.

It all started as a one-off match on Easter Sunday in the 1970s between the Bermuda-Irish and the Bermuda-English. The fixture quickly became an annual event, known as the

Easter Classic, where international players would fly in for a five-day stay on the island, culminating in the game on Easter Sunday.

The World Rugby Classic, where several of the top rugby nations were invited to participate in a week-long event was started in 1988. Over the years, the tournament has grown to attract the biggest names in the game in a celebration of sport and spirit. The island has also benefited with many local businesses and companies taking advantage of the corporate hospitality facilities on offer.

For me, though, the Classic is not just about the rugby. The festive atmosphere throughout the week really lifts the spirits. It is a throwback to the amateur days of rugby union, when the old tours united kindred spirits of all nationalities. It encompasses the social side of a game that demands commitment and concentration on the pitch, but friendship and camaraderie off it.

The Classic is generally played in the best of spirits, though there have been unsavoury incidents over the years as once-professional athletes struggle to get used to heavier legs and slower reaction times. Tempers occasionally boil over, but one particular incident that took place during the 2012 Classic springs to mind. I must stress again that incidents of foul play are few and far between, but this one stuck with me long after I left the island. I wrote about it soon after I returned to Ireland:

Saturday night, 10 November, the crowd at the National Sports Centre shrieks as the USA Eagles turn the ball over against the Springboks and sprint down the field. The Boks scramble to defend their line as the underdog Americans look to pounce for a try. A fumble on the ground brings a groan from the crowd and hands possession back to South Africa who clear the danger with a thumping kick. Leif Gibson, USA's thirty-four-year-old fly-half, turns his back on the opposition to trot towards the halfway line. Two seconds later, he is smashed from behind in the back of the neck and crumples to a heap on the ground. Later that evening, the doctors at King Edward Memorial Hospital say that he was lucky. The damage to his neck is not as serious as first feared. They confirm that he will be able to walk again, but that his rugby-playing days are over.

It's a dangerous pursuit, this wonderful game of ours. Rugby is entertainment for so many players and fans, but every so often we are served with a chilling reminder of the risks involved with playing the game. Contact sport is exactly that. Every player accepts and understands the dangers associated with participating in an activity where some form of physical damage is the norm rather than the exception. Rugby union carries some of the greatest potential for injury of any sport. Players accept the risks, even before a boot is laced or a jersey is pulled on.

Injuries happen every day. The laws of physics and biology demand that accidents are inevitable when two moving objects collide on a rugby field. There are rules and laws to limit the potential for injury, but no system is ever perfect and those who participate in rugby realise and understand that accidents are acceptable, if a little unpalatable. The word 'accident', as defined, does not allow for intent, and if there is no intent to harm, injury is just unfortunate. The situation changes altogether, however, when malice or intent comes into play.

The injury to Leif Gibson is one that sticks in my mind. A South African prop, six foot in height and weighing the best part of nineteen stone, smashed his elbow into the back of Gibson's neck. His motive for doing so still isn't clear but, whatever his reasons, there can be no justification for committing such a callous and brutal act on the field of play. He was arrested but no charges were brought against him. He also apologised profusely for his actions.

There is an unwritten contract that applies to every person who steps onto a rugby pitch. Each understands the physical dimensions of the game and accepts the consequences that come with playing their chosen sport. Over the years, I have watched thousands of players throw themselves into one another with little regard for their own personal safety. I've done it myself. But when someone crosses the line and turns tough physical play into common assault, it ceases to be about sport.

A team-mate of mine during my playing days at St Mary's made an interesting point after he retired from the game. He played the majority of his career with the same two props as a hooker in the front row. All three had seen and experienced their fair share of battles on the field and they grew to enjoy the physical exertions of competitive rugby.

Over the years, the men built and maintained a relationship based on trust and understanding. Each realised that their own safety and physical well-being was in the hands of the other two. If the props went down under the weight of a scrum, the hooker could be powerless to defend himself. As a unit, they stood or fell on the strength of their individual resolve.

They also relied heavily on the fairness of their opposition. Front-row forwards carry the biggest potential for serious injury because of the nature of their position at the head of the scrum. There is an understanding that your opposition has as important a role in ensuring your safety as your team-mates playing beside you.

Rugby is just a game. Players on the field will always strive for victory, but victory cannot come at any price. Sometimes, the line between intent to harm and accidental injury is quite thin, but in other incidents, the case is clear cut. Sport is as much about integrity and honour as it is about winning. Leif Gibson will recover from his injuries and for that, he is thankful and extremely fortunate. There are many before him who were not so lucky.

3. Leinster Schools Senior Cup

As a Corkman, reared in Munster, this one might raise a few eyebrows. When I was a kid at Pres Cork, all I wanted to do was to play for my school in the Munster Senior Cup. It was a burning passion of mine and I used to dream about scoring the winning try in the final or lifting the trophy in front of my classmates and friends. For kids in rugby-playing schools, the senior cup means everything. Those who are good enough to make the senior panel are expected to give up huge amounts of their time and energy to train three or four nights a week, outside of regular hours, in the hope of realising a dream. For most, the dream never happens. But the magic of the senior cup keeps them all coming back for more.

I've been living in Leinster for the best part of fifty years. During that time, I've been lucky enough to attend many schools matches and witness first hand the excitement and anticipation that surrounds the senior cup. For me, it is rugby in its purest form. These days, in every school, a huge amount of work goes into producing a senior cup squad, yet for the coaching and training that these young men undertake, they still manage to operate predominantly on gut instinct.

You can't knock the Rock.

Schools rugby is a very simple game. Players master the basic skills for their position and rely on whatever else comes to them on the day. It is genuinely the last chance to see this type of natural instinctive rugby before they move on to more regimented structures.

For me, the appeal of schools rugby lies in the players' natural ability. Too often these days, we watch professionals try and outwit each other in a drawn-out game of chess. There are so many coaches and technical analysts involved in top-tier sides that no stone is left unturned in identifying weaknesses in the opposition. Video analysis is a huge part of a coach's remit. And defences have become so tight and so complex that the attackers rarely get to express themselves to any meaningful degree. Rugby has become a sport structured on size and power. The slender, quick-footed back is fast becoming extinct, something I find genuinely upsetting. The modern game can also be quite ugly to watch at times. Schools rugby rarely is.

The Leinster Senior Cup has a tradition dating back to 1887 when Blackrock College were the inaugural winners. They have gone on to win the cup an incredible sixty-seven times, making them by far and away the most successful side in the competition. Rock's reputation precedes them. Every year, they begin the schools campaign as hot favourites and it is testament to the hard work and organisation of the teachers, coaches and students that they can keep producing sides that are capable of winning the title. Terenure and Belvedere College are a considerable way behind Rock with ten wins each, while Clongowes Wood College, despite success in a number of recent campaigns, have just eight wins to their name.

The Leinster Senior Cup has its critics, too. The competition has been dubbed elitist by those who point to fee-paying schools competing for the most talented players by way of scholarship offers or bonus tuition grants. There are claims of undue pressure being applied to players and coaches to deliver results. Whether or not you agree with any of that is pretty irrelevant as far as I'm concerned. It's difficult to argue against the critics but I tend not to bother and it does not stop me enjoying the games. And that's what I love about the senior cup. The rugby itself. I couldn't care less if Blackrock College or Clongowes Wood or St Michael's win the cup next year – it's all academic to me – I just enjoy watching the free-flowing rugby from some potential superstars of tomorrow.

RUGBY
1995
WORLD CUP

The International Rugby Board awarded the World Cup for 1995 to South Africa. It was the first time that the competition was held in one country and was also notable for the fact that it was the first major competition held in South Africa since that country was readmitted to the world sporting family following the dismantling of apartheid.

It was my third World Cup, and my third different involvement. This time, I was just weeks into a career of writing on rugby for the Irish Press Group. The newspaper asked me to travel to the tournament but pay my own way, with my costs being refunded on my return. However, between leaving Heathrow and arriving in Johannesburg, the newspaper shut down, and I was left at the tournament without a job to do and a big expenses bill, which I had no way of repaying. It did, however, have unintended consequences because I also did some work for RTÉ Television which eventually translated into a meaningful career.

The pool stages of the tournament were marred by the tragic injury to the Ivory Coast wing Max Brito. In the game against Tonga, he was catastrophically injured and paralysed for life. Sadly for him, after initial support from the competing nations, little was done to help him, and he remains a painful reminder to the International Rugby Board that the financial burden borne by disabled rugby players and their families is largely dependent on charitable donations. Brito, from an unfashionable and poor rugby nation, was soon forgotten.

As is customary, the pool stages went largely to plan. Western Samoa again qualified for the knockout stages and for the third World Cup in a row, Argentina made little impact. The most competitive pool was easily the one that contained New Zealand, Ireland and Wales.

Following the anthem debacle in 1987, Phil Coulter's 'Ireland's Call' made its debut at Ellis Park, Johannesburg. The composer was not entirely happy with the pace of the music but, for the first time, Ireland did at least have an anthem acceptable to both sides of the border.

Ireland opened the campaign against New Zealand and we had the first sight of the phenomenon that was Jonah Lomu. In a post-match press conference, the New Zealand coach was asked if he had seen somebody of that size playing rugby before. His reply was, 'Yes, but not on the wing.'

New Zealand coasted through the pool scoring forty-three points against Ireland, thirty-four against Wales and a massive 145 against a hapless Japan. That set up the crucial final game in Johannesburg between Ireland and Wales. Ireland won by a single point to reach the knockout stages and the management team of Noel Murphy and Gerry Murphy went to Durban with high hopes. Sadly it was not to be and, once again, Ireland returned from the World Cup without reaching the semi-finals, having been easily beaten by France.

The match of the quarter-finals was between England and Australia. It went down to the wire and Rob Andrew's winning drop goal from forty-five metres marked the first time that England had beaten the Wallabies outside of the northern hemisphere.

The penultimate stages of the tournament were notable for very different reasons. South Africa had a narrow victory over France in Cape Town, though the game was played

in appalling conditions, with parts of the pitch clearly under water and dangerous, and with most neutrals feeling that the game should not have been played. It was another occasion in the history of the Rugby World Cup where France were seemingly dealt a poor hand by the organisers.

New Zealand destroyed England in the other semi-final, in what was perhaps the greatest performance of Lomu's career. The match was over to all intents and purposes after twenty minutes when Lomu seemed to make it a contest between men and boys. He scored four tries in the match, most famously when Tony Underwood, Will Carling and Mike Catt all bounced off him on his way to the try line.

If one semi-final was controversial then the final was even more so.

The match went to extra time and a Joel Stransky drop goal was the difference between the two sides. After the match, there were allegations that the New Zealanders had been poisoned by a mysterious waitress called 'Suzie'.

However, against the iconic image of President Nelson Mandela in a Springbok shirt accompanied by the captain Francois Pienaar, nothing could dent the celebrations in the new 'Rainbow Nation'.

'Remember that
rugby is a team game;
all fourteen of you
make sure you pass the
ball to Jonah.'

Fax to All Blacks before 1995
World Cup semi-final.

Connacht have never lacked effort – as Tiernan O'Halloran shows – just recognition and resources.

93

3 PUNCHES THROWN AGAINST IRISHMEN

1. Nick Shehadie on Noel Murphy

Over the winter of 1957–1958, Australia toured Europe and came to Lansdowne Road in January. Up to this point, Ireland had not beaten a major test country, although, to be fair, at this point in their transition, the Wallabies were hardly a major test country. Both the Irish flankers – Jim Donaldson and Noel Murphy from Cork Constitution – were new caps.

Murphy was a month short of his twenty-first birthday but had become well used to the hurly-burly of forward play in the Munster Senior Cup. 'Noisy' had gained a reputation for being abrasive since his schooldays, and in this match he had a running battle with the Australian prop-forward Nick Shehadie. In his memoirs, Shehadie claims that Murphy was blocking his vision in this particular scrum, so he decided to take retaliatory action. In full view of the 33,000 people in the ground, Shehadie broke up from the scrum and levelled Murphy with an almighty punch.

Astonishingly, he was not sent off. His post-rugby career did not suffer either, as he became Lord Mayor of Sydney and was knighted by the Queen.

2. Brian Price on Noel Murphy

I was in the first week of my honeymoon in 1969, but was never going to miss the television viewing of Ireland v. Wales in Cardiff Arms Park on 8 March. Both teams were in the running for the Triple Crown, and Ireland travelled with high hopes.

At a maul early in the game, Brian Price, the Welsh second row, let fly at Noel Murphy with a devastating right hook that rendered the Irish flanker semi-conscious and dazed for the rest of the match. Like Shehadie a decade before, Price was not sent off. The British press were incensed, not because of the punch, but rather that it had

been delivered in full view of the Prince of Wales. *The Times* haughtily declared that 'it it was 'bad manners'.

Years later, Jimmy Davidson, who was the other flanker that day, told me that he felt that Price's punch had frightened his team-mates and that although the Welsh were a very good side, Ireland were mentally overcome by the ferocity of the physical exchanges.

3. Duncan McRae on Ronan O'Gara

During the 2001 Lions tour to Australia in the match against NSW Waratahs, which the commentary team described as a 'bear pit', Ronan O'Gara was repeatedly punched on the ground by Duncan McRae. It was one of the worst assaults in the modern game and even today the video makes nasty and upsetting viewing.

The Australian punched the Irishman more than a dozen times as he lay prone on the ground and O'Gara left the field with his face bloodied. McRae was duly sent off and the referee issued four other yellow cards, two to each side, so the match restarted with twenty-five players on the pitch.

Are the Lions tours good for rugby?

Traditions in sport change with time. Just as cricketers refuse to walk on appeal, soccer players dive in the box and Olympic athletes take drugs, the mores of modern professional sport are very different from the Corinthian ideals of Victorian times.

The Lions belong to an era when rugby touring was more akin to a public-school outing. Rugby tourists engaged in schoolboy antics, like getting drunk, chasing girls and wrecking hotels. The travelling press corps was complicit in the deal and reported none of the mayhem. The old phrase 'what goes on tour stays on tour' found its apogee in the Lions.

Today is very different. As we saw with the England team and its captain Mike Tindall in the 2011 Rugby World Cup, the 'dwarf throwing' indiscipline in a nightclub was instantly reported back home and the captain paid the price. However, as we saw during the 2001 Lions tour to Australia, players, such as Austin Healy, had ghost-writers for their newspaper columns back home to report every whiff of scandal from within the squad. It didn't need reporters to tell the story.

What made the Lions unique was that it had no equivalent in sport. The concept of four countries coming together to tour in a far-off land for months on end, forming friendships that would last a lifetime irrespective of class or creed, all the while testing their skills against the best in the world, has not been done in any other sport before or since.

The Lions cannot exist in the modern era for a number of reasons. First and foremost, the professional game can only be supported by massively increasing the number of international games in the off-season north and south of the equator. The result is that players are faced with a ten-month season.

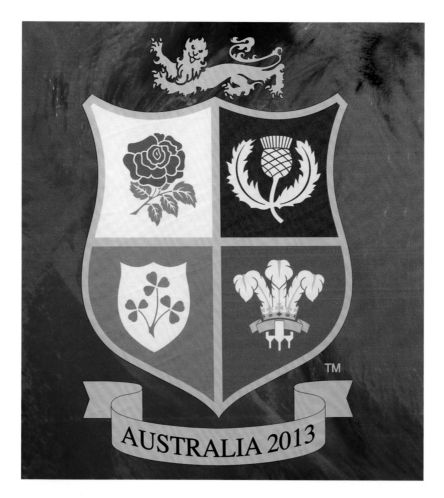

AUSTRALIA 2013

To fit in the periodic Lions tours, a huge change had to be made to the previous schedule of up to thirty games in the three-month period. Clearly, this is impossible, so the concept of short tours of a third of that length evolved.

Worse still, the pressure to generate revenue was such that Australia was awarded full tour status. Instead of being an addendum of four games to a Lions tour of New Zealand, the Australians were asked to provide opposition outside of the test matches, which was clearly beyond the abilities of a country where rugby was a minority sport.

The result was that most of the non-test games in Australia became walkovers and of no value. To make the tour viable, nonsense matches – like the game with the Barbarians in Hong Kong in 2013 – have been added. Even in New Zealand and South Africa, where rugby is the most popular sport, provincial games have been devalued by the omission of players in the test match squad. Thus, the great provincial sides, like Canterbury and Eastern Province, have become a shadow of the great teams of the past.

Three of the past four Lions coaches have also damaged the integrity of this great touring side. Graham Henry and Warren Gatland on their respective tours to Australia were mired in controversy about selection, style of play and treatment of non-test players.

For his odyssey in New Zealand, Clive Woodward was given unfettered powers and he brought more players, more coaches and more backup staff than ever before. The enormous cost involved was not attended by any success on the field. Astonishingly for a former Lion, Woodward broke with the great tradition of players sharing rooms in hotels. For me, his tour in charge marked the first step towards the demise of the concept.

It is no coincidence that the only tour in the past four that resembled the past in any small way was coached by Ian McGeechan, a man with a deep understanding of the history and traditions of the game.

To be selected as a Lion was once seen as the pinnacle of any player's career. When Warren Gatland brought Shane Williams all the way from Japan to play in a midweek game before returning home again, he made a mockery of the most prized shirt in world rugby. Players from the home nations on tour at that time in the four corners of the globe would happily have travelled to Australia to make a contribution.

The strength of Lions squads was always in the talent of players who did not make the selection or who were lucky enough to be called out during a tour because of injury to a squad member. Plucking Tom Court from a beach in Queensland had eerie memories of Paddy Wallace and Declan Kidney. That said, there is no way that Court was a legitimate candidate and, together with the Williams fiasco, it demonstrated that the Lions of the twenty-first century have no connection with their distinguished past.

A Lions tour is now merely a revenue-generating exercise, an excuse to sell replica jerseys and a boost to the tourist industry of the host nation. It is time to end what increasingly looks like a charade.

Hugh's View

Are the Lions tours good for rugby?

We adapt to change. History is filled with stories of successful people who built their fortune by moving with the times. Similarly, there are also plenty of horror stories recalling fortunes lost and lives destroyed by a steadfast refusal to bend to new rules. Accepting that change is inevitable enables us to do something about it. Clinging to the past will almost certainly result in regret.

The British and Irish Lions is not the same team today that it was thirty years ago. The game of rugby union has evolved considerably since the beginning of the professional era and life in the pro ranks today is very different from the amateur years. Those who still cling to the memory of the amateur era are blinding themselves to the joys of professional rugby.

Rugby has moved on. It is no longer a social activity requiring a small bit of physical exertion before the ultimate goal of making it to the bar. The days of playing for eighty minutes and then drinking for eight hours are long over. Committing to a rugby career today involves total and absolute dedication to a full-time professional sport.

Players today are bigger, faster and stronger than ever before. Defences are tighter and attacking space is more limited, but to suggest that skills are less prevalent than in the amateur game is simply not true. The players at the top of the game today are more skilful and knowledgeable than ever before. Fitness levels, too, are at an all-time peak and while the game has its problems, it has never been more enjoyable to watch.

For players today, life is very different. Weekly routines consist of brutal training regimes, abstinence, self-denial and a daily process of athletes pushing their bodies to the limit. Out-of-squad hours are spent resting, relaxing and recuperating. Every minute away from the training

Lions back row Tom Croft rises high to claim a lineout ball against Australia. The tourists went on to claim their first series win since 1997.

ground is designed to enable the body to recover sufficiently to absorb the impact of the next physical slog. It is an endless cycle of self-discipline.

Squad tours provide little relief. Players travelling abroad with club or country merely transfer their daily routines to the point of destination. The physical exertions remain the same and, environment aside, the daily routines alter very little.

The life of a professional rugby player requires those participating in it to spend the majority of their time with team-mates. These guys train, play, eat, sleep and travel together. They spend long hours in each other's company and they become each other's world. So, when an opportunity comes along to break from the normal routine, to experience life outside the bubble of a club or international squad, is it any wonder the players jump at the chance?

It is unfair to contrast the original concept of a rugby tour with today's definition. The goal posts have moved far too much for any comparison to be a fair one. I recently attended the Hay Festival in Kells, County Meath, where I had the opportunity to interview Welsh author and poet Owen Sheers on his new book, *Calon: A Journey to the Heart of Welsh Rugby*. Sheers spent a year in camp with the Wales rugby squad as they went from the heartbreak of a World Cup semi-final defeat to the glory of a Six Nations Grand Slam triumph in the space of six months. He immersed himself with the players and the management as the Welsh Rugby Union's first ever artist-in-residence. At the end of our talk in Kells, the audience had an opportunity to ask Sheers about his experience. Some of the questions hinted at late-night stories of player antics or the possibility of any humorous alcohol-fuelled incidents to garner a laugh – but there weren't any. Boring as it may have seemed, Sheers had none. The days of players going out and bringing back stories from nightclubs and bars while on duty, he explained, are over. They've been over for quite some time. It simply does not happen any more.

That doesn't mean a touring squad are incapable of enjoying themselves. Listening to Brian O'Driscoll speak during the 2013 tour of Australia, he commented on how much he enjoyed getting to know players outside of the Irish setup – players who for nine months of the year he was hell bent on breaking in half in club and international competition.

The Lions tour still affords players those kinds of opportunity. It brings countries together and unites them in a common sporting goal. It is perhaps the last remaining tie to the amateur era and while the minutiae of tour protocol have changed over the years, the concept and the overall ideal have remained the same.

The setup is not perfect and as with any professional tour, money rules. But the money does not get in the way of the rugby. And rugby is what the Lions is fundamentally all about.

Remember O'Driscoll's epic try against Australia in the first test in 2001? I never get tired of watching it – his vision, his strength and his pace to leave the Wallaby defence for dead. Fast forward four years and O'Driscoll experienced one of the worst moments in his career.

The great Willie John McBride before the 1974 tour to South Africa.

Minutes after leading the Lions out as captain, he was targeted and taken out by New Zealand's, Keven Mealamu and Tana Umaga. It ended his tour instantly and kept him out of rugby for months. He was lucky he wasn't paralysed. The Lions went on to lose all three tests in what is now regarded as one of the most disappointing Lions tours in history.

What about the 1974 Lions led by the great Willie John McBride that went unbeaten in twenty-two games to South Africa? The famous 'ninety-nine' call during that tour whenever the Springboks tried some rough-housing. I love watching clips of the great J.P.R. Williams sprinting from full-back to clobber Moaner van Heerden, fully in keeping with the 'one in, all in' mantra. And to top off the series, J.J. Williams' phenomenal try that started all the way back with Phil Bennett inside the Lions twenty-two.

There have been many more moments of brilliance and disaster in equal measure over the years. Each one part and parcel of the wonderful Lions experience.

Why should we discontinue a tour that is as popular today as it ever has been? People who love this game want to see a side with British and Irish players taking on the best that the southern hemisphere has to offer. Look at the number of fans travelling on the tour? Look at the capacity stadia throbbing with red jerseys at every test match, united in their cries of, 'Lions, Lions, Lions ...'

This tour must continue. It happens once every four years and it has its own special place on the rugby calendar. Let's not get sucked in to misplaced notions that the series is dominated by greed and commercialism. A Lions series cannot take place without proper funding and sponsorship, but the financial factors are only a means to an end. The end is rugby. Lions rugby. It must continue.

RIVALRIES

New Zealand V South Africa

One of the greatest rivalries in world sport is that between the rugby teams of South Africa and New Zealand. Because of the small number of first-class rugby-playing nations, these two countries competed more often than any other for many years. And, although the competition has always been passionate, nothing compares with the physical intensity of their games. The rivalry was also compounded by the political considerations off the field.

The first Rugby World Cup was played in 1987 and there have been seven tournaments in all. Australia, New Zealand and South Africa have each won the cup twice while England triumphed in 2003. As the Springboks were banned from the competition in 1987 and 1991 because of the government policy of apartheid, technically they have the best record in the tournament with two wins out of five appearances.

Prior to 1987, there was no doubt that the two best teams in the world were the All Blacks and Springboks and, with no world championship, these two nations competed for the unofficial mantle of being the world's best. Each country was desperate to win a test series and claim the title of world champions. In the amateur era, the Springboks won twenty-one tests to the All Blacks' eighteen. However, since the advent of professionalism, the All Blacks have held the upper hand.

The first test series between New Zealand and South Africa was in 1921. There were subsequent tours in 1928 and 1937, before the advent of the Second World War led to a hiatus. The first two series were shared but the Springboks won two of the three tests in 1937, outscoring their opponents by five tries to none.

When touring recommenced in 1949, Māori players were not considered for the tour of South Africa, lest the host nation be offended. It was a callow decision by the NZRFU given the enormous contribution the Māori people had made to New Zealand rugby.

The All Blacks were whitewashed in the test series, to the shock of supporters back home, as it meant that they had now lost two series in a row against South Africa. At that time, it was the custom to use home referees in the test matches and New Zealand returned home complaining bitterly about the standards of refereeing. It was to be a harbinger of even more protests seven years later.

At the time of the 1956 tour of New Zealand, South Africa had not lost a test series for sixty years. The series was to be the most brutal ever played between the two countries.

The Springboks were distressed by the amount of rough play they encountered and felt that the huge crowd support created situations where referees simply condoned illegalities by local teams. So strong were the emotions that just before the second test, the South African team management informed the NZRFU that they had decided to leave for home immediately after the game.

Having won the second test, the Springboks decided to stay in New Zealand, though the third test was to be the most violent. The All Blacks made seven changes from the losing team and lock Tiny White remembered that they were told that another loss would send the New Zealand economy into a tailspin.

South Africa possessed the two best props in the world, Chris Koch and Jaap Bekker. The New Zealanders picked former heavyweight boxer Kevin Skinner, suggesting that he was the best scrummager in the country. In truth, Skinner intended to take out the South Africans. This he did by punching them into submission, smashing Koch's face, which required eleven stitches.

The home referees were afraid to intervene and the games descended into mayhem. Years later, Springboks centre Ian Kirkpatrick remembered that he was accused of kicking Tiny White. 'I did not kick him, I missed,' he said. 'I just wish I had made contact.'

The eminent rugby writer T.P. McLean afterwards wrote when commenting on remarks by the secretary of the NZRFU that the All Blacks should prepare for the tests with hate in their hearts:

> By these and other signs one formed the impression that the country had lost its sense of proportion about the tour. Nor could one wholly blame the Springboks for feeling that they had been drawn into a holy war.

New Zealand finally won the series 3–1 but the ill-feeling persisted and, two years later, the Springboks at an IRB meeting threatened never to play New Zealand again. A rugby crisis was averted but four years later, the New Zealand tour to South Africa caused great offence when they decided again to travel without the Māori contingent. The Springboks won a close series to regain the pre-eminent position in world rugby.

In 1965, the Springboks were back down under and this time New Zealand triumphed on home territory. It seemed that these two evenly matched teams would continue to dominate world rugby and that the results would invariably go with home advantage.

New Zealand rugby finally discovers that human rights trump sport.

However, political storm clouds were brewing and in 1966 the NZRFU announced that it would not send a whites-only team to South Africa in 1967, and the tour was cancelled.

In the limited arena that was world rugby, the two major nations were desperate to continue contact and a replacement tour was organised in 1970. To placate protests at home, three Māori players and a Samoan, Bryan Williams, were selected. To overcome the apartheid regulations, they were treated as 'honorary whites'. For many New Zealanders, it was an insult. The Springboks duly won the series.

A change in government in New Zealand also meant a change in attitude and the new Labour administration postponed the scheduled tour until the team was selected on merit.

Then, in 1976, the All Blacks made what turned out to be their last official tour of white-ruled South Africa. The squad included five Māoris, plus Bryan Williams and, predictably, the Springboks were victorious.

South Africa was making cosmetic changes to its white-only selection policy and the 1981 squad included one black player. Although welcomed politically, the tour to New Zealand divided the nation and there were many violent protests. To this day, the match against NZ Māori is controversial. The Springboks drew the game with a disputed last-minute drop goal. Decades later, the kicker admitted that the ball had not cleared the bar, confirming the opinion of many Kiwis that the result was fabricated so that the Springboks would not be beaten by a team of black players.

The 1985 All Blacks tour to South Africa was cancelled at the last minute but twenty-eight of the thirty players selected from that tour decided to travel there a year later as part of an unofficial tour. Surprisingly, this squad contained eight Māori players. Argument still rages as to why Māoris travelled to a country that discriminated against non-whites.

In 1994, the first post-apartheid Springbok team toured New Zealand with just one non-white player. The visitors lost this series, but South Africa was now back on the world stage in sport and had been awarded the 1995 Rugby World Cup.

Memories of the 1956 tour surfaced when New Zealand alleged foul play after their defeat in the final of the World Cup – it was suggested that the players had been poisoned before the game.

The teams were to meet again four years later when South Africa beat New Zealand in the third-place play-off after the Kiwis had surprisingly gone down to France in the semi-final.

The great tours of the past are no more and these two powerful nations now compete annually in the Rugby Championship, the southern-hemisphere tournament. However, deep down, players and supporters from both countries realise that as the political landscape changes in South Africa, their ability to remain at the very top will become more difficult. Soccer remains the game of choice of the vast bulk of the black population in South Africa and the old Afrikaaner traditions, which have been at the root of the South African powerhouse game, are fading away.

3 TWICKENHAM DISASTERS

1. 1962

When I emigrated to London in September 1961, my first act was to join London Irish RFC. Not only did the club make me welcome but the friendships with so many other Irish people made living in London bearable. The following February, it did mean that I was able to get a ticket for Ireland's visit to Twickenham, though it proved to be a very difficult day for the men in green.

In 1958, Ireland had famously beaten Australia with five new caps in the pack. Four years later, the Irish selectors tried to repeat the exercise by picking five new caps in the forwards but added four new caps in the backs to make nine debutants in all, for a visit to one of the most inhospitable rugby grounds on earth.

At scrum-half, they picked a young man barely past his seventeenth birthday and partnered him with someone not much older. Johnny Quirke of Blackrock College was at number nine and Gerry Gilpin of Ulster at number ten. They, like the rest of their team, were overpowered by an English team with two-time Lions tourist Dickie Jeeps at scrum-half and the great Richard Sharp at fly-half.

Quirke, now a High Court judge, tells of standing in the tunnel and being advised by Jeeps, a durable Northants fruit grower, to make sure not to swap his jersey as he would always treasure it.

Although the Irish selectors were pilloried for a seemingly crass selection, it is interesting to consider some of the other players who made their debuts on that day. In the front row was the great Ray McLoughlin backed up behind by Willie John McBride and, on the flank, Mick Hipwell, who became a Lion in 1971.

During the game, Noel Murphy broke his collarbone but, as this was a time before substitutes, the Cork Constitution player played the remainder of the eighty minutes in what must have been excruciating pain. It certainly cost him his place on the Lions tour to South Africa later that year.

That season was also significant in that the Welsh game was postponed because of an outbreak of foot-and-mouth disease in Ireland. The game was refixed for 17 November and the Irish side coincidently had another nine changes, but this time there was no comparison with the team that had taken the field in Twickenham.

2. 1986

In the space of twelve months, Ireland went from the highs of the Triple Crown and the championship to four losses and being the dispirited holders of the wooden spoon. The nadir of the season came at Twickenham when Ireland were ruthlessly outscrummaged by England.

The London Irish loose-head Paul Kennedy had been selected for his first cap in Lansdowne Road against Wales when if his deficiencies in the scrum were not totally exposed, they were certainly noticeable to experts. However, in Twickenham he was destroyed and Ireland conceded four tries all directly related to a backpedalling scrum.

England had a debutante at number eight in the shape of Dean Richards of Leicester and he scored two tries by the simple expedient of falling on the ball over the line as the Irish scrum imploded. Ireland also had the embarrassment of conceding a penalty try at another scrum.

In an astonishing post-match interview, Mick Doyle suggested that there was nothing wrong with the Irish scrum, although for the next game against Scotland, Kennedy was replaced by Philip Orr in the only change in the pack.

The change made some difference but Ireland slumped to defeat by one point – 10–9 – to ensure that they finished bottom of the championship table without winning a match. It marked the end of what seemed the golden touch of Doyle and the coach exited the job after the disastrous 1987 World Cup campaign.

3. 2012

The suggestion that 'those who ignore history are doomed to repeat it' certainly holds good for the IRFU and the scrum. Irish rugby, which has given us Tom Clifford, Syd Millar, Ray McLoughlin and others, is now incapable at provincial and international level of putting out a scrum that can cope with the opposition.

A quarter of a century after the debacle of 1986, another disaster at the scrummage was witnessed in Twickenham. The Irish scrum although in trouble was surviving until the departure of Mike Ross, the Irish tight-head. He was replaced by Tom Court, a loose-head by trade who now had to fit in on the right-hand side of the hooker. The result was that the Irish scrum backpedalled even quicker than it had done on the self-same ground in 1986 and, like that year, conceded a penalty try at the set piece.

It was an embarrassment and once again Ireland was doomed to defeat by its inability to accomplish a simple task of locking out a scrum, something that had been meat and drink to generations of Irish forwards. It is surprising but true that with the advent of specialised and professional scrum coaches, Irish abilities in this area have diminished.

1999 RUGBY WORLD CUP

Wales were the hosts in 1999, but all the other countries in the Five Nations Championship hosted some of the games. The tournament was expanded by four teams to comprise twenty countries, which meant there were five pools of four teams. This, in turn, meant there was a play-off round for the five runners-up plus the best third-place team.

In 1999, world rugby could not support a tournament of twenty teams, and the gap between the strongest and weakest meant that there were some complete non-contests. New Zealand and England each scored over a hundred points against Italy and Tonga respectively. The bottom teams in each group conceded between 120 and 190 points each, and Uruguay and Spain have not appeared in the finals since 1999.

This World Cup was my first as a full-time television pundit. It was an extraordinary experience, which, in the dark days of my financial difficulties, I never imagined could ever come to pass.

My combined earnings between broadcasting and writing for the *Sunday Independent* did not amount to a great deal, but crucially, for the first time in thirty years, I had a real job and was bringing in an income.

It was at this point that my marriage to Ingrid started to become a real union. Over the years, she had watched me fritter away my time on rugby coaching and make a mess of my business life. Now, for the first time, she saw me using my rugby knowledge to earn a living. For my part, the battering my self-esteem had taken over the years began to dissipate and I felt that I had something to offer.

France, the best country never to win the World Cup.

Saturday, 2 October 1999 was a red-letter day in my life to that point. As I walked into Lansdowne Road for Ireland's opening game against the United States, the management of USA Rugby was arriving. Most of the group had been part of the committee that had sacked me as director of rugby just three years before.

I must confess that I ignored some of the proffered handshakes, as the hurt of our last meeting still cut very deep. It may have been rude, but I was a very different person from the broke and unemployable man I had been then.

Ireland duly beat the USA and Romania comfortably, but were no match for Australia which consigned them to a play-off against the best third-place finisher, Argentina.

In an ill-fated night at Lens, Ireland were embarrassingly beaten 28–24, and although it was to be over a year before coach Warren Gatland was sacked, that night in northern

France decided his future. The IRFU committee does not do embarrassment, and Lens was a night not to be forgotten.

The other matches went according to the seeding and the quarter-final line-up had a predictable look with South Africa, Australia, New Zealand and France all progressing to the semi-final stage. These two matches were both magnificent contests with Australia getting through after extra time against the Springboks.

Australia had gone into the game with only thirteen victories over South Africa in forty-four previous meetings, while the Springboks had not lost a World Cup match in nine appearances. Steve Larkham chose this match to score his first drop goal and did it from forty-three metres.

France reached another final by securing an astonishing victory over the All Blacks. The match ranks as one of the greatest in World Cup history. With New Zealand in front by 24–10, the result seemed a formality but in an extraordinary turnaround, the French scored thirty-three points to win 43–31.

In 1987, France had dismissed the favourites Australia in the semi-finals only to lose to New Zealand in the final; twelve years later, the French could not capitalise on their victory over the All Blacks and once again lost in the World Cup final. Australia were champions for the second time, but France, then as now, proved themselves to be doughty competitors.

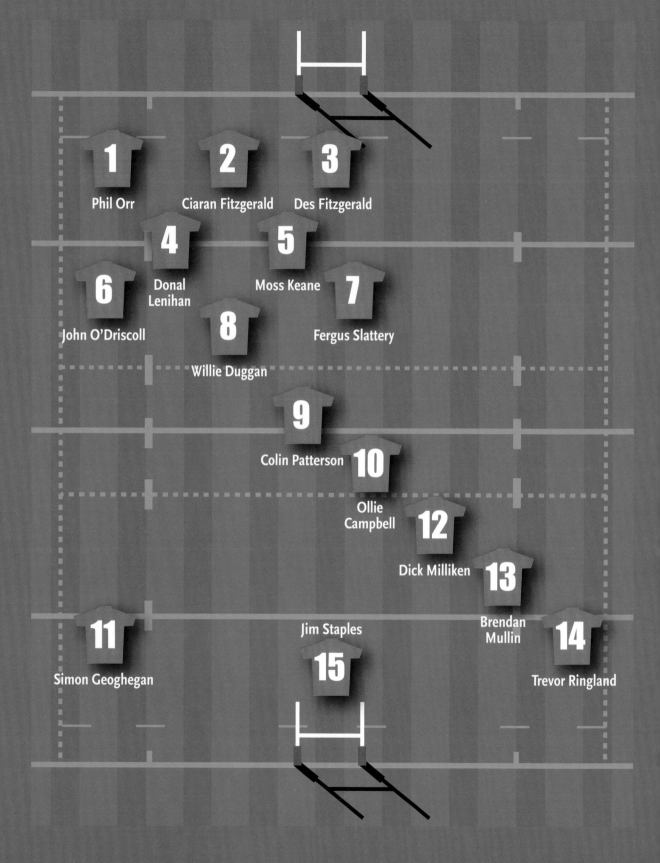

MY GREATEST IRISH TEAM 1974–1999

 Jim Staples

This period was a good time for Irish full-backs, though, for many, Staples may be a surprising choice. He makes the list based on his outstanding attacking ability, which was predicated by his pace. He was probably the quickest full-back of the era, his bravery was never exceeded and he was a secure tackler.

Honourable mentions:
Tony Ensor, Hugo McNeill and Conor O'Shea

 Trevor Ringland

With Keith Crossan, Ringland formed a powerful twin striking force, though they were two players of very different physical attributes and styles. Ringland used strength and power on his way to the try line and was a very difficult wing to defend against. With outstanding passers inside him, he would have been a major threat to any defence.

Honourable mentions: Richard Wallace and Tom Grace

Brendan Mullin

As a fourteen-second, 110-metre high hurdler, Mullin brought tremendous athletic gifts to the Irish midfield. He also had a keen understanding of the game and was a fine kicker. He did not have the most fruitful of relationships with David Irwin and Michael Kiernan – in fact, it was the arrival of David Curtis whose awareness gave Mullin greater space.

Honourable mentions: Michael Kiernan and Paul McNaughton

Dick Milliken

A severe ankle injury cut Milliken's career short but his selection here is based on his outstanding performance for the 1974 Lions in South Africa. Of his fourteen caps for Ireland, all but one were with Mike Gibson, with whom he formed a potent partnership in midfield.

Honourable mentions: David Irwin and David Curtis

Simon Geoghegan

The best Irish back never to make a Lions tour. By a combination of injury and poor selection, Geoghegan saw inferior players selected instead of himself. He was an outstanding attacking wing, full of pace and evasion. He famously completely confounded Tony Underwood twice to score tries. His enthusiasm for the game was matched only by his wonderful good humour. Every time he touched the ball, there was a ripple of excitement in the audience and few players chased kicks ahead with such commitment.

Honourable mentions: Moss Finn and Keith Crossan

10 Ollie Campbell

Campbell was the dominant number ten for this period, despite his short career. Paul Dean rivalled him as a passer, Eric Elwood as a place-kicker, David Humphreys as a line-breaker and Tony Ward as a punter, but no other fly-half had his range of skills and lack of a significant weakness.

Honourable mentions: Paul Dean and Tony Ward

9 Colin Patterson

Patterson was another player who had a short career – in his case from a bad knee injury – but a huge impact, and was easily the most exciting scrum-half for decades. Since the invention of the spin pass off an upright stance in the 1960s, Ireland has had very few outstanding passers. Patterson was almost the complete article and he remains one of the great losses to the Irish game in this period.

Honourable mentions: Robbie McGrath and Mick Bradley

8 Willie Duggan

Successful rugby teams always have at least one 'hard man'. In his time, Willie Duggan was not just the toughest man in Irish rugby, he may have been the toughest player in world rugby. He was part of a very unsuccessful Lions tour in 1977, but Duggan never gave up and took immense punishment on behalf of his team, which earned him the respect of his opponents. He ended his career after forty-one caps as the most unlikely captain Ireland ever had.

Honourable mentions: Brian Spillane and Noel Mannion

7 Fergus Slattery

Slattery was a quintessential open-side flanker. He had tons of pace, a strong tackle and a seemingly inexhaustible supply of energy. He was in New Zealand in 1971 with the Lions but failed to make the test side, a position he reversed in the hugely successful 1974 tour to South Africa when he played in all four tests. Although dynamic in the loose with the ball in hand, his one weakness was his inability to link up with support players. It was a tribute to his fitness and loyalty that he continued to turn out for his club Blackrock College at the very height of his fame and probably played more matches in that 1974 season than any other international of his time.

Honourable mentions: Nigel Carr and Shay Deering

6 John O'Driscoll

Off the field, the bespectacled pathologist from Manchester was mild of manner and softly spoken, but once on the pitch, he was insanely brave and intensely physical. He was the classic blindside flanker, and matched the hard men of New Zealand and South Africa blow for blow in six of the eight tests on two Lions tours.

Honourable mentions: Colm Tucker and Phillip Matthews

5 Moss Keane

Maurice Ignatius sounds like the name for a parish priest, but Lenihan's partner in the second row was not shy or retiring. He had a fantastic natural strength, which did not come from hours spent in a gymnasium. He never exuded fitness or mobility but few packs of forwards would have dismissed his selection. Despite his previous Gaelic football experience, he never seemed comfortable with the ball in hand. One suspects his average fitness levels left him out of position when the ball went free. Decades after Keane had finished playing, Ireland selected a prop-forward called 'the Bull', a name that could easily have been applied to Keane.

Honourable mentions: Willie Anderson and Brian Rigney

4 Donal Lenihan

Lenihan marked the switch from the old static scrum and lineout second rows to a more mobile version. However, as his career pre-dated lifting, he was adept at the hurly-burly in the contest for the ball thrown in from touch. He had good hands and in the limited continuity game then operating, he was a strong contributor.

Honourable mentions: Mick Galwey and Paddy Johns

3 Des Fitzgerald

Fitzgerald developed into one of the strongest prop-forwards of the amateur era through a strong weight-training regime in his teenage years. The excellent scrum coaching while at school in DLS Churchtown made him a fine technician. Fitzgerald was an old-school prop-forward, who concentrated on set pieces.

Honourable mentions: Mick Fitzpatrick and Jim McCoy

2 Ciaran Fitzgerald

Ireland has always been extremely strong at hooker, and this era is no exception. Fitzgerald stands out because of his captaincy and he would be the leader of this team. Hookers, like wing-forwards, come in different shapes and sizes. Under consideration were Steve Smith and Ross Nesdale who were big and strong, John Cantrell, Pat Whelan and John McDonald all fine technicians, while Harry Harbison was the best thrower at the lineout. Fitzgerald does not stand out under any criteria, but the overall package is strong when coupled with his leadership.

Honourable mentions: John Cantrell and Pat Whelan

1 Phil Orr

For a player who had major question marks against his scrummaging, his longevity at loose-head in the Irish front row gives some indication of his class. His value to the Ireland scrum was graphically demonstrated in the debacle at Twickenham in 1986, when he was replaced by Paul Kennedy before being promptly reinstated. He was the first of the highly mobile prop-forwards who was comfortable with ball in hand.

Honourable mentions: Tom Clancy and Nick Popplewell

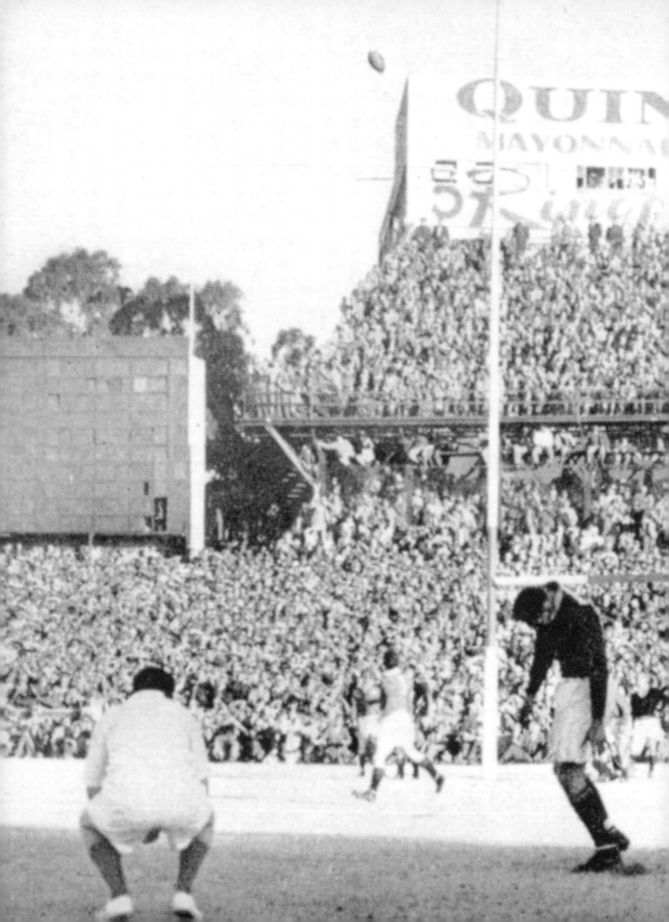

The kick that kindled my lifelong interest in the Lions. Jack van der Schyff misses the conversion and the Lions beat South Africa in the first test of the 1955 tour.

If ... the greatest Irish team played together

Sleep was slow coming, so I decided to close my eyes, lie back and think about how – perhaps in another world, in another place, at another time – all the great Irish players from history would somehow miraculously come together to play just one match. The problem, of course, was: who would be the opponents for this extraordinary fixture? Well, when you think about it, it can only be New Zealand. For this game, the All Blacks have picked the strongest side from their history, so it's going to be a titanic struggle.

For what purpose should this game be played? Well, there is only one charity that deserves the revenue from the turnstiles at this game; the money will be used for the reconstruction of Christchurch after the devastating earthquake in 2011. The first city of South Island and the second city of New Zealand may never be the same, but certainly the money raised from this match will go a long way to help restore this once-beautiful place.

Where is the game going to be played? At the insistence of the NZRFU, it is to be played at Carisbrook – 'the house of pain' – where New Zealand has played every other major test-playing nation. The All Blacks realise that they have a tough game on their hands and they have selected the ground because of its great tradition and, more importantly, for the fact that it is deep in Otago where the rain falls with great regularity. A wet, heavy ground will suit the

Tom Kiernan lines up the old Gilbert
ball for a toe-poke at goal.

home side. The official capacity at Carisbrook is 33,000 but like on so many other great test match days, almost 42,000 will cram into the ground, defying health and safety regulations.

Prior to the match, of course, laws and standards have to be set down as the players on both sides come from such different eras of the game of rugby union.

Tom Kiernan is not just the captain of this Irish team but his vast experience as a coach, and above all as an international rugby administrator, makes him the equal of the cranky Kiwis opposite him at the table.

The coach to the team is Ronnie Dawson who captained Ireland and the 1959 Lions and who was the first coach to the Irish national team. The meeting to decide the rules takes place over lunch, when Dawson, abstemious as ever, ignores the menu and has his usual wholemeal brown bread with mashed banana on top and a pot of tea. Kiernan knows that the coach's forensic and analytical approach to rugby will be a huge advantage. After all, had not Dawson devised the strategy for Kiernan to nullify the great attacking skills of J.P.R. Williams? And now he sits next to his captain as they debate the ground rules for the contest.

First and foremost, Kiernan wants to play with the modern ball and not the Gilbert of old. If it's going to rain, reckons the cute Corkman, we might as well have the best ball possible which will make handling easier. He gets his way as, after all, the hosts had the choice of country and ground.

There is a huge debate about the scoring methodology. The New Zealanders argue that the game should go back to basics with the try worth three points as of yore, working on the basis that the Irish are likely to score more tries. Kiernan is adamant and the argument rages for hours but eventually they settle on a compromise. It is to be four points for a try.

At this point, Kiernan is relatively satisfied with the discussion and raises no objection when lifting at the lineout is agreed. However, he is blindsided for the first time in his career when, in the spirit of cordiality, the canny New Zealanders suggest that for a match of this historical importance, yellow and red cards should be suspended. The Irish negotiation team reluctantly agrees given that Ireland has its own hard men who can match anything thrown at them in the close exchanges.

The rest of the details are sorted out fairly quickly. As per the modern laws, there will be no kicking direct to touch outside the twenty-two, however Kiernan is adamant in battling for a strict observance of the straight put-in at the scrum. He has been carefully prepared by Dawson and he makes his arguments cogently and, after a long wait, New Zealand eventually agree.

So all is set for the great contest.

The morning of the match dawns bright and sunny and everybody lucky enough to have one of the precious pieces of cardboard that will allow admittance to the ground is wandering around the ancient Scottish city of Dunedin in shirt sleeves. Brent Pope is giving an interview to world television and he suggests that the weather could change by kick-off time. Apparently, a cold front is heading towards South Island from Antarctica without any land mass to slow its course. There is a real possibility that the ground may become a quagmire, which will give the Kiwis a huge advantage.

However, by kick-off time, despite Pope's fears, or perhaps hopes, it remains dry but cold. The sod is firm and the respective supporters are in good voice. There are no anthems for this match but it starts with a minute's silence for all the great rugby players who will be watching in serried rows in the great rugby stadium in the sky. Kiernan wins the toss but elects to kick rather than choose ends because there is no perceptible wind advantage and he believes that getting into New Zealand territory as soon as possible is a good idea.

Kyle, whose drop goal had electrified Ireland and depressed Wales in 1956, starts the match. There is a full-scale follow-up by the men in green led by O'Connell, McKay and Murphy. Even the mighty Colin Meads who received the ball is driven to ground and trampled on unceremoniously. The stage is set; there will be no quarter asked or given.

Space does not allow for a full report of the game, but a synopsis of the major elements still makes compelling reading. The lineout was largely shared. Meads and McBride at the front ignored the lifters and concentrated on each other rather than the ball. There was little usable ball for the scrum-halves. However, Stringer and Going got much better value from the middle. Tiny White and Paul O'Connell hoisted high in the air, guaranteed the ball on the throw. However, at the back, Goodall and Kirkpatrick were having a massive battle. Fitzpatrick's throwing skills were superior to Wood and Ireland lost a number of their own lineouts as the ball went too high even for the towering Goodall. However, at the scrum, it was a different story. McLoughlin was making hay against Whineray, who was in terrible trouble. As he had done so many times in his career, the Kiwi captain called for some help from the second row. A fist came through and McLoughlin's nose spouted blood.

The scrum broke up in disorder but, unlike Canterbury in 1971, McLoughlin remembered to close his fist and Meads went down, poleaxed. The referee Gwyn Walters of Wales, immaculate in his blazer and shorts, delivered a stern lecture but he had no cards to issue. Meanwhile on the other side of the front row, Gray and Millar were having a running verbal battle. The All Black forward, who had fought a lifetime battle against the apartheid regime in

South Africa, asked Millar at every scrum where he was when the campaign to get one man one vote in Northern Ireland was taking place.

Going, forced to put in the ball absolutely straight down the tunnel, found that Keith Wood and company were able to win five strikes against the head, which more than made up for the losses at the lineout.

The battle of the back rows was like something from the Colosseum in Ancient Rome. Kirkpatrick was the dominant ball carrier on the field and Goodall time out of number was forced into making defensive tackles. Luckily for Ireland, Bill McKay foraged and fought for everything and this time there was to be no broken nose and concussion which had limited him in 1950. True to form, the two great try-scoring back rows in history, McKay and Kirkpatrick, shared tries in the first half.

However, when the teams went in at half-time, New Zealand led 9–4. The new ball although ideal for handling did not suit Kiernan's 'toe poke' style. In contrast Bob Scott, who before the game had warmed up by knocking the ball over the bar from halfway in his bare feet, had no problem readjusting. The Irish supporters in the crowd wondered if the selectors had made a mistake by picking a team without a world-class goal-kicker.

The first half had been an upfront battle. New Zealand with effectively two open-side flankers were winning the ball on the ground and the Irish backline was reduced to working off scraps; Noel Murphy was engaged in all kinds of nefarious activities in an effort to equalise the battle at the breakdown. True to his name, 'Noisy' engaged in a conversation with the players and the officials. He even commandeered the referee's mic to instruct the TMO to 'stop wasting bloody time and award the try' after McKay had grounded the ball while being tackled by Carter and Scott.

The Irish backline had been heroic against waves of attacks marshalled by Carter for the All Blacks. The out-half mixed his game between passing and kicking and time and again Kiernan was forced to make brave catches under pressure. Meanwhile Kyle, revelling in the unaccustomed space given him by the modern offside law, was judiciously keeping his outside backs in the game. The great fly-half knew that O'Driscoll and Gibson were marked men, so he worked the blindside linking with O'Reilly and Geoghegan. The blond and the redhead tested the much-vaunted Kiwi back three; while without the ball they never gave space to Kirwan or Jarden, who had scored so many tries in their careers.

Happily, although history does not record Kiernan's half-time talk – and, by the way, it took place on the pitch rather than in the dressing room – we did have an eyewitness in the young boy who brought out the oranges. The captain, his Cork accent, rising and falling under the emotional pressure of the biggest rugby match of his life, told his team what was required of them in this last forty minutes they would ever spend in each other's company in the green shirt of Ireland.

'Lads,' he said, 'have we come all this way to be beaten by a bunch of sheep herders? We have never beaten the arrogant shites and what better time to do it than now on their own bloody ground, in front of their own bloody crowd, playing under their bloody rules?'

He grabbed the shirt of his fellow Constitution man: 'Noisy, you were watching in 1978, you know they will cave in if we frighten them and tackle like Seamus [Dennison]. Jack,' he said, turning to his fly-half, 'you dominated them on this ground in 1950 and they only got a flukey draw because they had their own ref. Remind them, Jack, f✳✳✳ing remind them.'

If the good Protestant was offended by his captain's language, he did not show it as a slow smile spread across his face remembering his finest day in a Lions shirt.

The diminutive Peter Stringer happened to be standing between McBride and O'Connell. He was dwarfed by the two giant second rows and Millar, with his encyclopaedic knowledge of things African, thought to himself that it looked like a Bushman of the Kalahari flanked by two Watusi tribesmen. The Watusi are believed to be the tallest people in the world and descended, so the Bible story goes, from the giants who fled to Africa from Joshua's legions.

The captain eyeballed Stringer, 'Strings, let's cut out this recycling crap and get the ball into Jackie's hands as fast as possible so that we can use our advantage in the backs. I want Gibson to repeat what he did in 1971 and cut them open. Drico,' he continued, 'now it is payback time for Umaga; show them what they missed in Christchurch.'

The team gathered in a final silent huddle, each alone with his thoughts searching for a personal motivation that would make them deliver forty minutes of effort beyond the limit of human endurance.

Kiernan, remembering all those sunny afternoons in Cork when he would spend hours, after school in PBC, kicking a ball off the wall of Cork Jail with his brother Jim. McKay, the oldest in the group, remembering the friends he had left behind dead in the steaming jungles of Burma during the Second World War. He had survived and he made a silent promise to those fallen that he wouldn't let that chance of life that he had been given go to waste. The Ulstermen in the side who had stood to attention for two flags and two anthems for Ireland resolved to fight with the rugged independence of their Scottish forebears. Meanwhile the Munster players drew on all the slights, real and imagined, delivered to their province by countless Irish selectors.

The two wings were the calmest people in the group. In his head, O'Reilly was mimicking Whineray's accent and thinking of the jokes he would tell in the after-dinner speech. Somehow, Geoghegan had smuggled a Walkman and ear buds on to the pitch and had missed his captain's impassioned speech as he listened to some rock music. Doctor McKay had found the irrepressible Londoner impossible to understand, and wondered if the young man had St Vitus' Dance, the movement disorder, as he watched Geoghegan's head nod up and down.

Wilson Whineray – average prop but great captain.

The promised rain held off in the second half – it was if the Almighty wanted to see the famous green shirts remain loyal to their great traditions of running the ball. At every ruck, Stringer screamed for quick ball and fired passes to Kyle that seemed to owe their origins to a .22 rifle. Kyle barely had time to draw breath, but as he stood at every set piece, he could not help but remember the eleven scrum-halves who had partnered him in his forty-six-match career for Ireland.

The space afforded him by the bullet-like passes and the change in the offside law made it seem like a stroll in the park. Within minutes, the Irish number ten glided outside the despairing hand of McCaw and jinked off his left foot inside Carter thirty metres from the Irish try line. He did not have to look because the youngster, whose long hair and wispy beard had so offended the conservative Gibson, was at his shoulder.

The short pass was given and O'Driscoll was free and clear. There was still an enormous amount to do as full-back Scott was aided and abetted by the fast-covering Kirwan. Seemingly without effort, O'Driscoll launched a long pass that put O'Reilly en route to the line. The wing, with wonderful good looks that were rumoured to have earned him a screen test for *Ben Hur*, was no slouch when it came to scoring tries in the southern hemisphere. His long legs unhindered by abbreviated shorts ate up the ground and he scored at the corner with Jarden a poor second. Kiernan missed the conversion, but there was only a point in it at 9–8.

The balance at the breakdown had been redressed. O'Driscoll was now competing on the ground with a frenzy that astonished all six back rows on the field. Suddenly Ireland were the equal of McCaw and Jones – but the Kiwis were not going to be outdone in a part of the game they considered their own. They rucked with abandon buddies in green and black shirts were indiscriminately rolled back as the ball came to Going like a hen laying an egg. The rucking was brutal but intensely fair, there was never a hint of a stamp and the studs were always facing backward, not downward. O'Driscoll, taking huge punishment, continued to slow down New Zealand ball.

New Zealand continued to inch ahead with two Scott penalties while Kiernan failed with a long-range effort from halfway.

Carter, realising New Zealand possession was slow, used all his kicking skills to keep the territorial advantage. It paid off as a succession of driving rucks close to the Irish line saw Meads crash over next to the posts for a try and give Scott an easy conversion.

With twenty minutes to go, New Zealand were thirteen points clear and seemingly coasting despite wonderfully inventive back play by Ireland. The New Zealand defence seemed impregnable until Wood made a buccaneering run from halfway and set up three consecutive pick and go drives by O'Connell, McBride and McLoughlin. This sudden change in tactics from quick delivery at the ruck confused the All Blacks' defence.

At the third time of asking, McLoughlin laid the ball back for Stringer, who rifled a left-handed pass to Kyle who was twenty-five metres from the line and faced by four primary defenders. In a magical reprise of Ravenhill in 1953, the fly-half stepped inside and outside the four men in black like an Argentinian dancer doing the paso doble. His break had brought him closer to the corner flag than the goalposts, but Kiernan was equal to the challenge and made his first successful kick of the afternoon.

Ireland still needed to score at least twice, as time ticked away. Kyle was now mesmerisingly efficient and Carter could only stand and admire. Slashing breaks by O'Driscoll and Gibson seemed sure to finish in tries but somehow the New Zealand defence held out.

During a break in play while an injury to one of the All Blacks was seen to, Kiernan sauntered up from the back with the distinctive splay-footed walking style to talk to Kyle. The team, in the true tradition of the game, had only met the day before for a ninety-minute practice session when there had been little time for complicated backline moves.

'Jackie,' said the captain, 'let's try that move with myself doing dummy runs in the middle and O'Reilly coming around from the blindside wing.' The game restarted with an Ireland scrum forty yards out on the right-hand side of the field. It was not ideal for Stringer as his back would be to Kyle if Wood delivered a fastball down channel one of the scrum.

The ball duly arrived, the scrum-half hit the out-half, Kiernan, and Gibson ran towards the right-hand touchline. O'Driscoll took the ball from Kyle, and the hugely threatening figure of O'Reilly entered the line off the blindside. The defence was fixed and O'Reilly gave the ball to Geoghegan with twenty metres to go and Kirwan to beat.

Just as he had done to Tony Underwood all those years ago at Twickenham, the flying

'Where's your f***ing pride?'

Londoner went inside and outside his opponent before doing precisely the same thing to the finest full-back New Zealand had ever produced and scored in the corner.

Kiernan, ever the pragmatist, knew he was having a bad day at the office and handed the kicking duties to Gibson, who could not improve.

It seemed all too little too late as the clock inched towards eighty minutes. As the Irish lined up to receive the restart, somewhere in the crowd, a lone Irish voice rose above all others. The words were indistinguishable, but they were soon taken up by the Irish men and women around the ground, all of whom knew that soulful renditions of 'The Fields of Athenry' would not be enough to lift this team. The New Zealand crowd was stunned as they heard thousands of Irish voices shout as one, 'Where's your f***ing pride?'

Carter knew that his drop-out was crucial. If he could keep Ireland deep in their own half, the match was won. His left-footed kick was inch perfect, but O'Connell was equal to the task and riding high on the hands of McLoughlin and Millar, he plucked the ball out of the sky like a Kerry midfielder on an All-Ireland Sunday. From the ruck, McCaw was penalised and Kyle punted to the halfway line.

Now came the great strategic dilemma that had dogged Irish rugby for over a century. Three points would give a very creditable draw, and within the team they were players who believed that driving forward and waiting for the drop goal that had epitomised Munster's great success over the years was the way to go.

Others like Gibson and O'Driscoll believed implicitly in their ability to beat any defence in the world. At the lineout, Stringer looked to Kyle, seeking direction. Kiernan stood fully thirty metres back in the centre of the pitch and did not voice his opinion – he knew that this decision had to be made by the greatest rugby footballer Ireland had ever produced.

Stringer passed on the message to Wood. Carter warned Umaga and Robertson to be ready for the inevitable thrust up the centre. The hooker threw the safe ball to O'Connell and then peeled around as Kyle had surprisingly instructed. The ebullient Wood crashed through Michael Jones and headed straight for Carter.

That ruck was won and Murphy took the ball on from Stringer's short pass to create a second ruck. Kiernan could not believe the plan. 'Jesus, he cannot be going for a drop goal,' lamented the captain, realising that the out-half had only kicked one drop goal in his entire international career.

At that ruck, Kyle had brought the entire backline around to the right. He took Stringer's pass and ran diagonally towards the touchline. Sensing danger, the bulk of the All Blacks moved to cut off the threat. But one player on the Irish side remembered Swansea in 1951 and moved towards the centre of the field instead.

Kyle launched a towering cross-kick and Bill McKay, just as Jim McCarthy had done all those years ago, safely pouched the pig skin and touched down under the posts. The conversion was academic. Ireland had beaten New Zealand for the first time.

At the post-match dinner, a slightly inebriated president of the IRFU offered the team their choice of transport home. Murphy remembered how Niall Brophy and Mick English had travelled home in 1959 after injury had shortened their tour. Before captain or coach could speak, the flanker piped up, 'We will take the boat.'

Ireland:

Tom Kiernan (c); Tony O'Reilly, Brian O'Driscoll, Mike Gibson, Simon Geoghegan; Jack Kyle, Peter Stringer; Syd Millar, Keith Wood, Ray McLoughlin, Willie John McBride, Paul O'Connell; Bill McKay, Noel Murphy, Ken Goodall

New Zealand:

Bob Scott; John Kirwan, Bruce Robertson, Tana Umaga, Ron Jarden; Dan Carter, Syd Going; Ken Gray, Sean Fitzpatrick, Wilson Whineray (c), Colin Meads, Tiny White; Michael Jones, Richie McCaw, Ian Kirkpatrick

10 GREAT IRISH TRIES

1. Jackie Kyle v. France, 1953

I just wish I'd been there to see the try that is still spoken of in hushed tones by people who did see it. The match was played in Ravenhill because, in those years, Belfast and Dublin shared the home international matches. Kyle took the French defence apart and I can remember well as a schoolboy reading the *Sunday Independent* the following day and seeing a wonderful picture of Kyle coming off his left foot to beat a French defender. In that try, he beat more than one defender and it ranks as one of the great tries in Irish history. The *Sunday Independent* headline writer excelled himself by quoting from Baroness Orczy's *The Scarlet Pimpernel* with the lines:

> They seek him here, they seek him there
> Those Frenchies seek him everywhere.
> That paragon of pace and guile,
> That demned elusive Jackie Kyle.

2. Noel Henderson v. Australia, 1958

This game was my second visit to Lansdowne Road for an international, this time it was to be against the touring Australians whom Ireland had never beaten. The captain of the Irish team was Noel Henderson, who was coming near the end of his career. Like his friend and fly-half Jackie Kyle, Henderson was a product of Queen's University. Surprisingly, for a player who had won a test place for the Lions on the wing, he was viewed to be lacking in pace. That day, he was partnered in the centre by David Hewitt, making his debut at the age of eighteen. The youngster passed to Henderson in space on the halfway line and the big Ulsterman set off on the lung-bursting run to the line. With all of Ireland willing him on, he made the try line and sealed Ireland's win.

3. Pat Casey v. England, 1962

You may wish to watch this on YouTube with the voiceover from yours truly. And I can do no better than paraphrase what I said during that commentary about this great try, which completed the demolition of England at Twickenham by eighteen points to five. 'Even the forty-year-old camerawork and the black-and-white images cannot disguise the great quality of this try. Mike Gibson's great break gives us a glimpse of what a great fly-half he might have been had he not become an even greater centre. He linked with the late, Jerry Walsh, a much underrated centre, who then passed to Pat Casey for one of the great tries of this or any other era.' What made it really special was that all the passes utilised a switch by the receiver. It started inside the Irish twenty-two and ended under the English posts.

4. Ken Goodall v. Wales, 1970

My first visit to Lansdowne Road had been in 1956 when Wales had come to call with a Five Nations title beckoning. They were sent home with their tails between their legs after an extraordinary performance by Ireland, culminating in a drop goal by Jackie Kyle from the touchline. However, by the time Wales came to town in 1970, seeking a second successive Triple Crown, Irish rugby supporters had become used to being beaten by them. However, on that trip, the visitors disintegrated and Goodall rounded off the victory with a solo try from near the halfway line in what was to be his final game in rugby union. He picked up a loose clearance kick and chipped over Barry John's head. He then caught the ball on the bounce, charged past Gareth Edwards and J.P.R. Williams and crashed over for a try. Tom Kiernan's conversion made it 14–0 and the Welsh were beaten.

5. Gerry 'Ginger' McLoughlin v. England, 1982

Ireland's Triple Crown year may well be remembered for this try, although the contribution of Ollie Campbell to the title was immense, scoring forty-six points in that championship season. Campbell was also crucial to this great try. It all started with a fairly predictable short penalty move outside the English twenty-two where Campbell had a drop-goal attempt blocked down. However, Ciaran Fitzgerald regathered the ball and passed to Campbell who set off down the blindside and linked with Fergus Slattery, and was on hand again to receive the pass and, brilliantly under pressure, found Willie Duggan. The number eight transferred to McLoughlin ten yards from the line and the Limerick man went over 'festooned with Saxons'. It should be remembered that Campbell's conversion from the touchline was vital as Ireland won 16–15.

6. Noel Mannion v. Wales, 1989

This may even be a greater number eight try than Goodall's nineteen years earlier. Mannion was the first international from the Corinthians club in Galway and was an outstanding talent. He had wonderful hands, great pace and a keen appreciation of the game. Following a successful lineout, Wales were in full flow heading towards the Irish twenty-two when Bleddyn Bowen, the fly-half, attempted a left-footed chip, which Mannion charged down. However, the Connacht player did much more than that, he hung on to the ball and set off on a run towards the line seventy metres away. He was chased all the way by the Welsh open-side David Bryant, but made it to the corner in Cardiff for a superb individual try.

7. Gordon Hamilton v. Australia, 1991

Ireland have never made the semi-finals of the Rugby World Cup but at Lansdowne Road in 1991, they were ten minutes from just that achievement. In a seemingly innocuous move, Jim Staples broke out of the twenty-two and kicked ahead, but wing Jack Clark won the physical battle with David Campese. Clark picked up the ball on the run to carry the move forward. Open-side flanker Gordon Hamilton had made a seventy-yard run from the breakdown to appear on Clark's right. He took the pass and went over at the corner, despite Rob Egerton's despairing tackle, for one of the great tries in Ireland's World Cup history. Fly-half Ralph Keyes converted and a nation went wild. Sadly, Campese was to destroy Ireland's hopes but Hamilton will never be forgotten for that amazing try.

8. Simon Geoghegan v. England, 1994

In the early 1990s, Connacht, London Irish and Eddie O'Sullivan had a big influence on the Irish back play. Jim Staples, David Curtis and Simon Geoghegan had worked with Eddie at club and province where they had concocted a back move called 'Sullivans'. Even though Staples and Curtis had departed the national scene by 1994, the move continued. It needed the full-back and the centre to make dummy runs while the blindside wing entered the backline. In Twickenham, it worked perfectly as Richard Wallace came off his line to pass the ball to Simon Geoghegan, but the blond wing still had it all to do. Facing him was Tony Underwood, the pride of England, who was turned inside out by the speed and evasion of Geoghegan's running and the Londoner went over in the corner for a famous try that ruined England's hopes of the Triple Crown. Interestingly, it was Ireland's only win of that championship.

9. Shane Horgan v. England, 2006 and 2007

I could not separate these tries as they are both classics of the winger's art.

In Twickenham, with time running out, O'Gara chipped delicately from a scrum on his own twenty-two, the ball bounced kindly for Brian O'Driscoll who careered towards the English line. It is often forgotten just how quick Shane Horgan was for a big man and he flew down the touchline on O'Driscoll's right. The centre's pass seemed

certain to put Horgan over but he was stopped just short of the line. There followed a succession of Irish rucks before the ball went right to Horgan five metres out, where he was faced by Lewis Moody, the English open-side. Despite the Irishman's bulk, all the advantage was with the Englishman, but Horgan managed to crash through the tackle to score. After an interminable wait, the television match official awarded the try.

A year later, England were again the opponents, this time on a hugely emotional occasion in Croke Park. The match wasn't much of a contest, but Horgan's try from a perfectly placed O'Gara cross kick was the highlight of the afternoon. The wing had to show courage in the air, great hands and, above all, an elastic arm to down the ball just inside the corner flag.

10. Brian O'Driscoll for the Lions v. Australia, 2001

O'Driscoll had made his debut for Ireland two years previously against the self-same opponents at the Gabba in Brisbane. He was now back in the iconic red shirt and being partnered by his team-mate Rob Henderson. They were an unlikely partnership

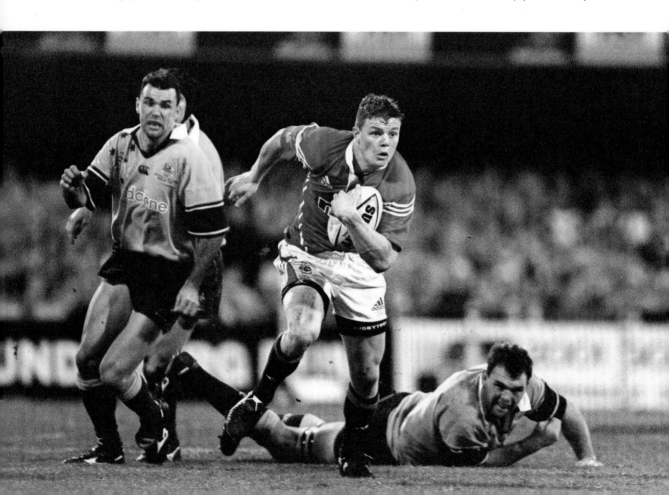

before the series started, but their form on tour had made them an automatic choice for this match.

For the first test, the roof was closed, multiplying the noise of the Lions' supporters. The Australian Rugby Union was surprised at the size of the travelling support and, in fact, in the subsequent two tests, made it a distinct policy to separate the visiting fans in the stadium in order to dilute the noise. O'Driscoll announced himself on the world stage with the magnificent try, taking a short pass from Jonny Wilkinson and cutting a devastating line through the massed Australian defence. He showed tremendous pace in open field and then made a bewildering sidestep to leave the last Australian defender for dead, before touching down under the posts. The young man demonstrated what were soon to become his trademark skills. He could run wonderful lines and angles, had fierce acceleration and he could beat a defender off either foot. We had witnessed the arrival of one of the greatest players the game would ever see.

RUGBY
2003
WORLD CUP

The 2003 Rugby World Cup was set up for one of the three southern hemisphere countries to win, but England spoiled the party down under and stole the Webb Ellis Cup from under everyone's nose. Clive Woodward oversaw a campaign that maximised England's strength up front and Jonny Wilkinson's super-human ability to kick goals. It wasn't pretty to watch, but it was extremely effective rugby. Wilkinson's match-winning drop goal against Australia in the final was like something out of a fairy-tale. Ireland's campaign read like a bad romance novel.

Looking back now, I believe it's quite possible that Alan Quinlan was single-handedly responsible for prolonging Eddie O'Sullivan's international career by four years. It's ironic really, given Quinlan's treatment under O'Sullivan during his playing career, but you could make a case that Quinny's try against Argentina in 2003 saved the coach's neck.

Ireland began their 2003 World Cup pool campaign with comfortable victories over substandard opposition. Tries went in from all angles as Romania (45–17) and Namibia (64–7) both failed to put up much of a fight. Ireland went into their third fixture against Argentina relatively unscathed.

It was just as well. The Pumas had been threatening to break into the top eight of the IRB world rankings for some time, and they saw Ireland as the perfect opportunity to prove their value to the international game. It was a gruesome but entertaining battle at the Adelaide Stadium, with both sides trading blows over eighty long minutes in the Australian heat. Argentina went ahead early on with a penalty from Quesada before Quinny popped up for

his superb try. The Shannon man had forced his way into the team for the Pumas match on the back of a two-try haul against Romania and he was itching to take his chance. Quinlan was never shy about fronting up in the physical battles and he seemed to relish getting stuck into the opposition faces and causing as much havoc as he could. He was picked specifically to do a job against the grizzled Argies and, for a short time, it worked perfectly.

With eighteen minutes on the clock, Keith Wood pounced on a poor Puma lineout to break over the halfway line and sell a wonderful dummy to the Argentina defence. Quinlan, with seven on his back, ran like a mad demon to support his captain and took a pass on the outside before crashing over to score to the left of the posts. It was a bitter-sweet moment for the Munster flanker who dislocated his shoulder in the move and played no further part in the campaign.

That try proved decisive. Ireland added the conversion and a penalty from David Humphreys before two more penalties from Ronan O'Gara secured a very uncomfortable and hard-fought 16–15 victory in front of a crowd of just over 30,000. The Argentinians limped off the pitch in disgust at their own performance, but for Ireland this was sweet revenge for the shock defeat to the Pumas four years earlier. Eddie O'Sullivan advanced his army to the final pool game against Australia where a top finish in the group was up for grabs.

They almost pulled it off. Ireland dominated possession (53 per cent) and territory (55 per cent) on 1 November 2003, but they just couldn't find a way to convert those statistics into points. Ronan O'Gara had an off day with the boot, missing three from six kicks at goal before being replaced by David Humphreys in the second half. But Australia were always in front. A first-half try from flanker George Smith and six points from the boot of centre Elton Flatley gave the Wallabies an 11–6 lead at the break. They went further ahead early in the second half when Flatley struck another penalty, but Brian O'Driscoll scored a magnificent try in the corner to narrow the gap with O'Gara slotting the conversion for a 14–13 scoreline, but it wasn't to be Ireland's day. An exchange of penalties between the sides left Australia one-point winners at the Telstra Dome in Melbourne, 17–16. It was heartbreaking for O'Sullivan to watch his side dominate one of the World Cup favourites only to come off second best. But there was no time to dwell on the result, as that defeat left Ireland in the runners-up spot in Pool A. A quarter-final against France beckoned.

It was always going to be an extremely difficult task to take down the French in Melbourne. France had coasted through Pool B with hardly a hair out of place, putting sixty-one points past Fiji and fifty-one past both Scotland and Japan. Les Bleus were scoring tries for fun and had a dangerous, confident swagger as they went about their business. Ireland were merely another obstacle to be negotiated and France wasted little time putting points on the scoreboard. They ran Ireland ragged and were out of sight by the half-time whistle with tries from Olivier Magne, Christophe Dominici and Imanol Harinordoquy contributing to a 27–0 lead. Ireland fans could only watch in horror as the men in green were out-muscled, out-thought, out-manoeuvred and out-played. There was simply no way back. A brace from Brian O'Driscoll and a Kevin Maggs try put some small respectability on the final scoreline, but France were simply awesome and ran out comfortable 43–21 winners after eighty painful minutes. Yet again, Ireland's World Cup campaign was finished at the quarter-final stage.

The 2003 campaign swung disastrously on the back of that defeat to Australia in the final pool game. Victory over the Wallabies would have seen Ireland advance to a quarter-final match against Scotland. Instead, they drew a France team full of confidence and in devastating form. The narrow loss to Australia was difficult to take – there were too many silly and unnecessary penalties in key positions. It was as if they never really believed that they could win.

England sailed through their own pool with wins over South Africa and Samoa to guarantee their pace in the last eight. They accounted for Wales 28–17 in the quarter-final before going on to topple France 24–7 in the semi-final. During those two games, Jonny Wilkinson scored an astonishing forty-seven of England's fifty-two points. That statistic only reinforced the view that England had based their campaign on ten-man rugby. It was pretty dull to watch, but it was also incredibly effective. Australia, despite home advantage and a surprise semi-final win over the pre-tournament favourites New Zealand, couldn't prevent Wilkinson from kicking England to glory in the final at the Telstra Stadium in Sydney. His drop goal in extra time secured a 20–17 win and ensured Martin Johnson became the first captain from the northern hemisphere to lift the Webb Ellis trophy.

George's View

Who is the greatest Irish player of all time?

John Wilson Kyle won a then world record forty-six caps for Ireland between 1947 and 1958. In those eleven seasons, he missed only four games through injury and otherwise was an automatic choice. Only in his retirement was he known as 'Jack' – to a generation of rugby supporters all over the world, he was 'Jackie'. His place in the annals of Irish rugby were cemented when, in 2002, he was named by the IRFU as the greatest Irish rugby player of all time and, in 2008, when he was inducted into the IRB Hall of Fame.

Kyle made his debut against France in Lansdowne Road eighteen days after his twenty-first birthday. He was a medical student at Queen's University and it was the first official international after the end of the Second World War. Because of the eight-year interruption because of hostilities, there were fourteen new caps in the Irish side – only full-back and captain Con Murphy had played in the pre-war era.

When measuring Kyle's performance against a modern-day number ten, it is important to understand the offside law of the time. Offside was determined not by the hindmost foot, but by the ball. Also at the scrum, the flanker could disengage and stand facing the fly-half. Kyle and his contemporaries were faced with the defender less than five yards away.

Kyle's greatness stands not just on his performances for Ireland, but particularly on the 1950 Lions tour to New Zealand. He is still considered by that country as one of the greatest players to have ever toured there and he was named as one of the six players of that year by the *New Zealand Rugby Almanack*. It is a testament to the extraordinary talent of this Irishman that he was judged in New Zealand as the finest attacking fly-half they have ever seen.

Astonishingly, Kyle played in twenty of the twenty-nine games on that tour. He scored a hat-trick against West Coast and Buller. Three tries are unusual for any individual, but Kyle is the only Irish fly-half in history to do it. When you consider the defensive alignments of the time, it is even more extraordinary. On that same tour, his performance in the first test in Dunedin was magnificent. The match ended nine points apiece, but Kyle scored a try, made one for wing Ken Jones and forced a penalty, kicked by John Robins.

The attrition of Lions tours is immense and only four players played in all four tests in 1950. Kyle was the only three-quarter with a 100 per cent record which was a testament to his fitness when you consider that, in five weeks of the tour, he played in both the weekend and midweek games.

For Ireland, his performances never dropped below the outstanding. Some highlights were the manner in which he masterminded the Grand Slam season of 1948, the outstanding individual try against France in 1953, his drop goal from the touchline that beat Wales in 1956 and his tactical kicking, which was vital in the defeat of Australia in 1958.

Kyle was a consummate defender in the manner of his era. With the law allowing the flanker to stand so close to the opposing number ten, Kyle's job was to cover cross-field towards the corner flag and make many of the last-ditch tackles that, today, we associate with

the full-back. He was brave to a fault. In 1958, as Australia threatened to sink an Irish team playing against the wind, time and again Kyle made courageous marks to deny the opponents.

He was cruelly treated in 1955, when an arbitrary decision was made by the Lions selectors not to select anybody over the age of thirty for the tour of South Africa. Ireland had a bad season in the run-up to the tour, failing to win a match in the Five Nations Championship. However it did not prevent Robin Thompson being selected as captain and teenagers Tony O'Reilly and Cecil Pedlow going as three-quarters. Second row Tom Reid and hooker Robin Roe made up the Irish contingent.

It is difficult to compare players of different generations. It is even more

Balance, focus and technique.

difficult to compare players of the amateur and professional eras. However, the following elements of Jackie Kyle's personal life and rugby career should be borne in mind when considering his status in Irish rugby history:

1. From the age of thirteen to nineteen, crucial years in the development of a rugby player, the Six Counties as part of the UK were at war with Germany.
2. From 1939 to 1950, food rationing would have been in place.
3. The laws of the time favoured the defender against the fly-half.
4. The Gilbert leather ball, when wet, had the handling qualities of a bar of soap and the weight of a slab of concrete. It made handling and kicking immeasurably more difficult than today. When punting, unless the ball was struck perfectly, it could be extremely painful.
5. He was not a place-kicker, because the convention of the time was that the full-back took penalties and conversions. In fact, because of the aerodynamic qualities of the ball, prop-forwards were often very successful kickers.
6. Training was part-time, while Kyle qualified as a doctor.

Kyle is chaired off the field by Ronnie Kavanagh and Noel Henderson having established a new world record of forty-five caps. He would earn just one more before his rugby career was arbitrarily cut short.

149

Who is the greatest Irish player of all time?

What makes a rugby player great? It's a question I ask myself every time I sit down to watch a game. Each match brings with it the small possibility that the next rugby genius will reveal himself to the world and even if it doesn't happen right there and then, there will always be another game not too far away. In a sport that entices the quick, the strong and the clever, what does it take to stand out from the pack? What are the attributes necessary to make it to the elite level?

Some people have greatness thrust upon them and Brian O'Driscoll is one such person. His rise to rugby superstardom did not happen by accident, but there is something almost coincidental about his time on the rugby field. The reason I say this is because to watch O'Driscoll play is to witness a man operating almost entirely out of instinct. His gut reaction every time is for the spark of genius that will unlock a defence or the bone-crunching tackle that will dislodge an opposition ball. He stands out amongst his peers because he is prepared to do what few others are for the good of his team. Again, there is no deliberate thought process to this because, in international rugby, timing relies on split-second decision-making. It is where players stand or fall, and O'Driscoll is the most naturally gifted and instinctive player I have ever seen.

Ever since 2000 when he burst onto the international stage with that phenomenal hat-trick in Paris, O'Driscoll's skill and appetite for the game has captivated fans the world over. He truly is a phenomenon. It is so rare to watch a player who possesses such a varied and finely tuned skillset. Flankers the world over have lauded his application and bravery at the breakdown while wingers and centres of slightest foot have been left flummoxed by his pace and trickery. O'Driscoll was never the quickest player on the field but his balance, poise and acceleration off the mark have left many faster legs flat on their feet.

His triple whammy against the French in 2000 was breathtaking to watch. In the cauldron of aristocracy that is the Stade de France, he never flinched once. The Parisian crowd could only admire this young kid who carved open the France defence with such ease. To strike once in Paris is fortunate. Twice is plucky, but three times? *Sacre bleu!*

As for career highlights? There are far too many to recount in full. Who could forget that magnificent solo try for the Lions in Australia in 2001? The then twenty-one-year-old took a pass inside his own half and flew past Wallabies hooker Jeremy Paul, rounding the Australia full-back Matt Burke to touch down for a sensational score. It was the moment the world sat up and took notice.

At the time of writing, O'Driscoll has amassed 125 caps for his country, scoring forty-eight tries. He has six Lions caps, three Heineken Cup titles with his club Leinster and has been voted Six Nations player of the championship on three separate occasions. He was also *Rugby World* magazine's player of the decade in 2010.

And then there is the man himself. Fame and fortune have led many grounded souls off the path of congeniality and onto higher planes, but not O'Driscoll. His deference and honesty is an example to any aspiring sports star that the realisation of talent does not have to mean the absence of humility. As an interviewee, he has remained engaging and thoughtful in the face of all manner of intonation, and while it can't have been easy growing up as one of the poster boys of Celtic Tiger Ireland, O'Driscoll's integrity and charm never has wavered. He is the perfect example of excellence on the sports field and, I imagine, a pleasure to know off it.

It is difficult to put O'Driscoll's influence on Irish rugby into context. To say that he is the greatest I have ever seen is to leave a gaping hole in his resumé. I have watched him topple giants, round wizards and fend off dragons over a fourteen-year career. To achieve 125 caps in the professional game requires a resilience and toughness that perhaps few really understand. The game has changed so much over the past twenty years that fans today can spend an entire season watching players putting their bodies on the line, week in week out, and think nothing of it. It's almost expected. The physical reality of what the players put themselves through today won't be fully understood for many years to come.

In this regard, I worry for O'Driscoll's future health. Some of the hits he has taken would put a car off the road. His hardest tackles defy the laws of physics and biology. Who can forget his bone-crunching smash on South African Danie Roussouw during the 2009 Lions tour? Roussouw stumbled like a drunk man as he fought to regain his composure. He had just been tackled by a man four stone lighter and six inches smaller, and he didn't know where he was. O'Driscoll got up and played on. Over the years, the Leinster centre has disregarded his personal safety on countless occasions. I just hope he does not come to regret it.

The unfathomable decision by Declan Kidney to strip O'Driscoll of the Ireland captaincy before the 2013 Six Nations Championship was as insulting as it was ludicrous. To watch O'Driscoll play rugby is to witness leadership of the highest calibre. Players gravitate towards him because he is prepared to go one step farther than anyone else for the good of his team. Kidney's bizarre call ultimately started his own downfall as Ireland coach. O'Driscoll deserved better than that.

We are nearing the end of an exceptional rugby career. There cannot be many more matches left in Brian O'Driscoll. I wish we could all watch him line out for Ireland in the 2015 World Cup, but it looks like that achievement may be beyond even him. His absence will leave an unquantifiable void in Irish and world rugby but perhaps only when he is gone will we truly understand the value he brought to the game in this country.

For me, he is not only Ireland's greatest player, but perhaps the greatest I will ever have the pleasure of watching in my lifetime.

A battle-scarred Brian
O'Driscoll holds off three
Munster players to deliver
the pass in another
instalment of Irish
rugby's greatest rivalry.

10 GREAT IRELAND CAPTAINS

1. Karl Mullen

Contrary to popular belief, Mullen was not captain of the Ireland Grand Slam team in 1948 – at least he did not captain the team in all four matches. The first game of the season was against France in Paris and the captain was scrum-half Ernie Strathdee, who was dropped for the next game against England enabling twenty-two-year-old Mullen to take over for the next three successive victories to claim the championship, the Triple Crown and the Slam. What made Mullen special was that there was no backup. He was the coach, the manager and the organiser. Most of the players on the team would have been older than him, including two veterans of the Second World War, J.C. Daly and Bill McKay. As captain, he delivered one Grand Slam, two Triple Crowns and four championships. Amazingly, after an unbeaten season in 1951, he was replaced as captain by Des O'Brien. Mullen also captained the outstanding Lions team to New Zealand in 1950.

2. Tom Kiernan

When asked why Kiernan was not selected for the Munster Schools team, the chairman of selectors, a priest from Rockwell College, replied, 'Because he is too cute by half.' The good cleric did not realise the truth of his observation – Kiernan had a razor-sharp mind which made him an outstanding player, captain, coach and administrator. When he retired, he was the player with the most caps, the highest points score and most games as captain in Irish rugby history. He is the only Irish captain who bears comparison with Mullen. Like Mullen, he captained the Lions, in his case on the 1968 tour to South Africa. His coaching record includes Munster's victory over the All Blacks in 1978 and Ireland's Triple Crown in 1982 and, as an administrator, he was a powerhouse in the discussions on professionalism.

3. Ray McLoughlin

Professionalism and coaching have diminished the role of the captain, therefore it is not surprising that the top choices in this list come from the amateur era. McLoughlin is placed remarkably high, given his short sojourn in charge and the fact that he never captained the Lions. He first captained Ireland against France in 1965 and brought his huge intellect to the job of leader. He was immediately successful and in his first season went to Cardiff with a Triple Crown to play for and, although that game was lost, there was a real sense of direction about Ireland. South Africa were beaten 9–6 in Lansdowne Road a month later. McLoughlin, the independent-minded captain, was never popular with the IRFU and it was not surprising that his tenure ended after just three more games. Once described as the greatest technician in rugby union, he was a huge influence on the forward tactics in the successful 1971 Lions tour to New Zealand.

4. Ronnie Dawson

It is a testament to Dawson's leadership that he could successfully captain the 1959 Lions tour to New Zealand and Australia while in many people's opinions he was not the first-choice hooker. Like Kiernan and McLoughlin, Dawson was a huge rugby

intellect and an outstanding leader of men, as is witnessed not just by his captaincy skills but by his performance as coach to Ireland and the Lions. Like many others, he suffered the indignity of losing the captaincy but continued to play for Ireland for three more years. With Kiernan and Syd Millar, he provided immense stature on the IRB that gave Ireland a disproportionate voice in the affairs of world rugby.

5. Paul O'Connell

Only two modern players make the captaincy list, primarily because, for much of the time, the role of the captain has been taken over by the large management groups that now support teams at provincial and national level. O'Connell's position is secured by his extraordinary leadership during Munster's performances in the knockout stages of the Heineken Cup. The professional captain is very often chosen from the best players rather than the best leader: O'Connell during the 2009 Lions tour in South Africa demonstrated strong leadership in difficult circumstances. On the other hand, at Munster he led from the front as a player.

6. Brian O'Driscoll

This may seem an astonishingly low position for a man who has captained Ireland on so many occasions but, in my view, O'Driscoll was given the captaincy too early in his career, based purely on the fact that he was the best player. Furthermore, his period as captain of the Lions was cut short by a terrible injury, but the fact that he was overlooked as captain for the tour to South Africa in favour of O'Connell indicates that not everybody shared the view that captain was his natural position. His great strength is loyalty. He is loyal to every coach he has worked with – sometimes under very difficult circumstances – but O'Driscoll has never wavered in his support. It is obviously difficult to assess his behind-the-scenes performance as captain, but he has never demonstrated a strong on-field tactical direction like most of the great captains.

7. Ciaran Fitzgerald

Fitzgerald had a very strong career as captain of Ireland, delivering two Triple Crowns and the championship, as well as captaining the Lions in New Zealand in 1983, and he played at a time when Ireland were very competitive at hooker. John Cantwell and Pat Whelan were probably better technicians but Fitzgerald had leadership qualities. They were recognised by coach Tom Kiernan when he surprisingly handed Fitzgerald the armband for the opening game of the 1982 championship. The result was a Triple Crown followed by a championship when the team only lost one match, to Wales. At that point, Kiernan had departed and been replaced by Willie John McBride as coach, and the team disintegrated to a wooden spoon. Fitzgerald survived, though McBride didn't, and the captain delivered another Triple Crown under Mick Doyle. He was also captain of the Lions in 1983 when he handled a barrage of criticism by the British press with outstanding fortitude and good manners. The tour was a failure, but few captains in Lions history faced such a difficult task.

8. Willie John McBride

One may well ask how can the man who made five Lions tours, who would be on most people's all-time great player list and who remains an iconic figure in the game forty years after his retirement rank so low in the list? He took over at Ireland late in his playing career and his selection as captain of the Lions on his fifth tour begged the question: why not earlier? McBride was a captain who led by example rather than direction. With the Lions in South Africa, he was lucky to be surrounded by some of the best players ever to wear that legendary red shirt. He was further helped by coach Syd Millar, who was at the very peak of his powers and devised a major strategy to defeat the Springboks. However, even with his successes, McBride was a much better player than a captain.

9. Keith Wood

Of the three hookers in this list, Woody ranks third as a captain but certainly first as a player. Like others, he led from the front and never counted the cost of his physical endeavours. One sensed that he was often too involved in the game to think about the strategy of the match, as for instance in his lineout calls. He was also a hugely influential figure on two Lions tours as a player.

10. Donal Lenihan

Lenihan succeeded Fitzgerald as captain and was eventually himself replaced by Phillip Matthews, whom he served loyally as a player. History will be kind to Lenihan, as he was much underrated as a leader. His performance as captain of the Lions midweek team, christened 'Donal's Doughnuts', demonstrated the kind of commitment that was part and parcel of Lenihan's character. It would have been easy as a non-test selection to coast along through the tour, as many had done before him. He was also Ireland captain, in the inaugural World Cup of 1987, when Mick Doyle was at the nadir of his career. Similarly, Lenihan never let up when Doyle's successor, Jimmy Davidson, had his own difficulties as coach.

The end of refereeing as we know it

If there was a world championship for referees, Ireland would probably win it nine times out of ten. Since the Second World War, Ireland has consistently had a referee in the top six of the world rankings.

As far back as 1948, the great Ham Lambert, who had played cricket and rugby for Ireland, was recognised as one of the best referees in that championship. Ray Williams was so good that when the All Blacks toured these islands – and in those days, remember, the touring side could choose the referee – they asked to have Williams to officiate at almost all of their international games.

In the 1960s, Kevin Kelleher was the outstanding referee of his generation and courageous enough to send off Colin Meads for a wild fly-hack at the scrum-half. This was in marked contrast to what happened when Paul O'Connell was guilty of a similar incident. Dave Burnett was also similarly courageous in sending off Paul Ringer of Wales. It is important to understand that Kelleher and Burnett refereed in the amateur era when sendings-off were comparatively rare, and they did not have the benefit of input from the touch judges. Other Irish referees, like John West, Owen Doyle and David McHugh, have proved that Irish refereeing is second to none.

Paul Ringer discovers that Dave Burnett
takes no prisoners.

The common thread is a complete absence of fear when making a decision. These referees have never been influenced by politics, career advancement or indeed the baying voices in the crowd. There is another vital aspect to referees and it is an understanding of what the players are trying to do, and a willingness to allow them to express themselves on the pitch.

In the professional era, the role of the referee has changed dramatically and not necessarily for the better. Let us look at some of the innovations. The referee is now in microphone contact with his assistants, and many of the decisions are made by the man running the line rather than the man theoretically in charge of the match with the whistle. Decisions on tries are made by the television match official, or TMO, as a result of referees being unwilling or unable to take responsibility. Even when the try is obvious to the naked eye, there is a rush upstairs for confirmation rather than risk making a mistake.

The International Rugby Board has now decided to extend the role of the TMO to incidents of foul play and judging whether or not passes early in a move that led to a try were forward. Thus, the referee may call for a decision on a pass that took place on the halfway line that was followed by seven exemplary passes, two sidesteps and a blistering run to the line for the touchdown.

The game is now certain to be held up for inordinate lengths of time as decisions are referred upstairs. Rugby union, which has inexorably followed rugby league in its approach to the number of defenders strung out across the pitch, is now set to rival its transatlantic cousin and have games that will last well over two hours interspersed by television replays that will no doubt give sponsors commercial opportunities.

The effect on refereeing and referees will be dramatic and fatal. The next generation of referees will have grown up officiating in a game in which every decision made by them will be open to question by the television camera, and they will simply be unwilling to take any risks.

Comparisons have been made with cricket and the use of the video replay. There are pluses and minuses in this comparison. Cricket is already a very lengthy exercise, but the actual decision referred to the camera is very short and, by and large, does not require a great number of camera angles – so the decision on an LBW, for instance, can be made very quickly. The big positive of the cricket system is that the call for a disputed decision is made by the captain, and as he is allowed just two challenges, he will very often not use the option if he feels that the decision was right in the first place.

Rugby if it intends using camera technology more might well benefit from such an innovation. The proponents of video technology will cite the case of Thierry Henry and his handball against Ireland in Paris. So what! Sport has always been about disputed decisions and the story, probably apocryphal, of the Welsh forward on his deathbed still claiming that he had scored the try that would have won the match for his country against New Zealand is part of the charm of the game.

Irish referee John West was not very popular in Wales because he made a number of decisions during his career that went against the Principality. It never stopped him from making tough calls and, like Williams before him, he was chosen by touring sides to officiate. My own personal coaching history might well have been very different had Owen Doyle in my first interprovincial as coach to Connacht against Munster not awarded a drop goal to Ralph Keyes that was wide and disallowed a drop goal by Eric Elwood that was good. Instead of an unlikely victory, we were condemned to a brave defeat by a single point. Today, Doyle and I are still friends and I bear him no ill will, because he made those decisions without bias and certain in his own mind that they were correct.

The game is now bedevilled by less-than-courageous referees, who simply perform to tick boxes on an assessment form, established by the IRB and used by an assessor (invariably a former referee), sitting high in the stand. Thus, every single international game has a free kick for early engagement at the first scrum. It is irrelevant whether or not there was early engagement, it is so the referee knows that he has ticked a box.

Elsewhere in this book, I have referred to the ignoring of the crooked feed at the scrum by modern-day referees. The officials know that this is countenanced by a higher authority and, therefore, continue the practice of placing a good law in disrepute.

If one wants to see the idiocy and inanity of the modern approach to the laws of the game, then one only needs to go to YouTube and look for 'Total Rugby – Forward Pass' to see that it has reached the point of no return. Using scientific gobbledygook like 'relative velocity', it makes the decision on a forward pass impossible for a referee and sets back every decision made under that law for the past 150 years.

Every week this year, we have seen widely divergent decisions being made by referees. In the Heineken Cup, Paul O'Connell was adjudged – quite wrongly by referee Nigel Owens – to have passed the ball forward. Meanwhile a couple of weeks later in the semi-final of the RaboDirect, Alain Rolland ignored what appeared to be forward passes by Ulster. Judged by the old laws and the new science of physics, as applied to the law, Ulster had a case to answer.

The forward pass in rugby may quickly follow the crooked feed at the scrum into oblivion. It is not beyond the bounds of possibility that as television executives put increasing pressure on rugby administrators to provide a game that is easier for the watching public to understand and more exciting as a spectacle, the pass forward, as exemplified in American football by the quarter-back, could be part and parcel of rugby union a decade from now.

In the 2011 World Cup final between France and New Zealand, the home team were under enormous pressure in the last quarter. In that period, the number of penalties awarded to France was minimal, although many observers have suggested that the reverse should have been true.

In a blistering attack on Craig Joubert, the referee of the final, Neil Francis and Matt Williams on television demonstrated a large number of occasions where a penalty might have been awarded to France. Right or wrong, the pundits made a very strong case. In that final, Joubert was under extraordinary pressure in front of a home crowd in a rugby-mad nation where winning the World Cup was seen as part of the nation's economy.

The more decisions that are taken away from referees and handed to video evidence and scientific appraisal, the more the quality of people aspiring to be international referees will diminish.

Rugby referees used to come from the ranks of retired players, which invariably meant that they took up the task when in their thirties. However, because they had played, they invariably had a deep understanding of the difficulties experienced by players in the tackle, at the breakdown and in the scrum. They had, or at least the best ones had, what was called 'a feel for the game'. In those days in club games, the referee changed in the dressing room of one of the teams, as few clubs had separate accommodation.

Time and again on Saturday afternoons one could judge by the expressions on the faces of the players as the referee came through the door whether they considered that they had 'a good one or a bad one'.

The problem for retired players in seeking advancement to international level as referees was that they were beginning a new career at a time when their physical abilities were diminishing. Thus, Irish international referees like John West or Owen Doyle had either retired early or not played the game at all. Importantly, they were young enough and fit enough to keep pace with the demands of international rugby.

In the professional era, Alain Rolland is a rarity, in that he played international rugby for Ireland but luckily, as far as a refereeing career went, he retired when he was still quite young. It is possible that his playing experience has made Rolland the outstanding referee in world rugby that he is today.

In contrast, Wayne Barnes of England has managed to upset all the major countries in world rugby at some point or another. He is, as Gilbert and Sullivan might have put it, 'the very model of a modern major referee'. Barnes referees like the lawyer he is and it is no coincidence that he has reached the top of the refereeing profession because he fulfils all the criteria demanded by his masters at the International Rugby Board.

There are a few advantages to growing old, but I am happy that I will not be around to watch the great game of rugby union become a television spectacular, played by gladiators and refereed by people using television monitors.

This brave new world of rugby will have front rows built like sprinters because there will be no need to hold up the scrum as the scrum-half will, with impunity, put the ball in to the

Alain Rolland – the best in the world.

feet of the number eight. The games will last three hours, punctuated by long delays while videos are consulted to make decisions on tries, forward passes and foul play. To keep the audience happy during the breaks, scantily clad ladies will move around the crowd selling lottery tickets and beer. Over the public address will come pounding rock music interspersed with lunatic contributions from a former darts commentator.

A bit far-fetched you may say, but the changes proposed to the refereeing of the game will have to be accompanied by changes in the laws. The sport's need for money to pay for the ever-increasing bureaucracy to regulate the game, together with the cast of coaching, playing and refereeing will mean that television producers will become increasingly more important in determining what the public sees.

To gain the greatest audience, television must dumb down the sport. That is why, today, there are more forms of abbreviated cricket being played than the traditional five-day test match.

The change in refereeing standards heralds is the first but crucial step towards ending the game as we know it.

George's View

Should Ireland have a sevens team?

The worst thing for the game of rugby union is the increasing popularity of seven-a-side rugby and its acceptance into the Olympic Games in 2016.

The abbreviated game was developed in Melrose, Scotland, where the annual Melrose Sevens tournament is still played. It was always intended to be an end-of-season diversion and took a long time to gain popularity outside Scotland – Ireland has never been enamoured with the sport.

The sevens tournaments in Leinster during the 1960s and 1970s were for junior clubs or the second teams of senior clubs and played on consecutive weekends. The CYM tournament was held at Anglesea Road on Palm Sunday and the following Sunday, North Kildare hosted an event. For a short while Old Belvedere flirted with a senior tournament with invited foreign teams.

Meanwhile the Galwegians tournament took place on Easter Monday. Many teams played in North Kildare on Sunday, danced and drank until a late hour before a quick few hours sleep in Corscadden's Hotel to prepare for the trip to Galway on the Monday.

Probably because of the lack of a sevens tradition, and more importantly because the IRFU recognises the threat posed by this new international game, Ireland do not enter any of the tournaments played worldwide. However, Ireland's women have been very competitive, including the 2013 Sevens World Cup series in Moscow.

Medal sports in the Olympics receive substantial funding from the IOC so, after 2016, small countries with little or no opportunity of breaking into big-time rugby union will be adequately funded. That means that countries like the United States who are on the periphery of world rugby will be tempted to concentrate on sevens.

Even Portugal can compete in sevens rugby.

The problem for the US Eagles is the supply of good coaches and the difficulty of producing world-class set pieces. At a stroke, those problems go away if sevens rugby becomes the primary sport. Coaching is relatively easy – scrums and lineouts are not under pressure – and the only skills required are to run, pass and tackle. Does anybody doubt that the USA can find ten big men or women who can run fast, tackle like trucks and make a short pass to supporting team-mates?

In 2013, Carlin Isles ranked thirty-fourth among US men in the 100 metres, but has become a star of the sevens circuit despite having no experience of rugby. The 10.3-second 100-metre man is the fastest man in the condensed game and demonstrates how the USA could be a force in the 2016 Olympics without any talent in the conventional rugby sense.

The same applies to all the minnows of world rugby. One only needs to look at the results in the famous Hong Kong Sevens to see the emerging nations in this sport. Portugal, which does not merit a fixture at any level against the major countries, performed with distinction.

The problem for the big eight countries is that there is already a highly congested fixture list, so the top players do not perform on the world sevens circuit. Thus there is no Dan Carter for New Zealand, Leigh Halfpenny for Wales or Morgan Parra for France.

Ireland does not have the player pool to support the national team and the provincial sides as well as taking perhaps as many as twenty players out of the mix to prepare for tournaments, and ultimately the Olympic Games. If Ireland were to enter the games in Rio de Janeiro, then the Irish public would have an expectation of seeing Rob Kearney, Tommy Bowe, Jonny Sexton, et al. – and this is simply never going to happen.

The problem would become even more dramatic at schools level. The ethos of sport in school is participation. Prioritise sevens rugby and the number of available places on the school team is cut from fifteen to seven. More importantly, there would be no place for slow kids, overweight kids and kids with poor hand–eye co-ordination. All the reasons that make rugby union such great sport for schoolchildren will be lost.

Even more importantly, if sevens is the main activity in schools, where will the future prop-forwards, locks and scrum-halves come from? Scrummage technique must be learned at a young age, the ability to box kick will be lost and the throwing at the lineout will disimprove further.

The advantages are clear. Because there will be fewer soft tissue and orthopaedic injuries, insurance costs will plummet, making the game very attractive to schools and clubs. There will be similar savings in the cost of hiring coaches, as only at the top level does coaching have any significant input.

Television will love the new sport as the entire game is over after twenty minutes and it is easily understood by the audience. It is interesting to watch the crowd at these tournaments. Because the game requires little attention span, trips to the bar are absolutely essential.

Tournaments are seen as fun days out and eccentric costumes, Mexican waves and partying are part of the deal. Even on finals day, there is no real sense of intense competition other than that between the players involved on the pitch. In order to survive, sevens has to be a travelling circus; the serious component of the sport is lost.

There is a real danger that the momentum for this sport together with the huge success of Tag Rugby will mean that rugby union will become a minority sport played by gladiators for television.

The great traditions of the game designed for hooligans but played by gentlemen may be lost forever and will be the final blow to the endangered species that is club rugby in Ireland.

Hugh's View

Should Ireland have a sevens team?

Ireland must compete on the international sevens circuit and the fact that it does not have any representation at the moment is farcical in the extreme. It is also extremely damaging to the development of the game here. The skills needed to compete at the top level of IRB sevens competition – speed, power, skill and stamina – are all transferable to the fifteen-a-side game. There are plenty of reasonable arguments in favour of setting up a national sevens squad and very few logical reasons against it. When will the IRFU take its head out of the sand and address this issue as a matter of priority?

The professional game is getting tighter with every passing year. Players are getting bigger and the amount of space for attackers to exploit is diminishing with each season. Extensive video analysis and blitz defensive systems have cut down on the amount of time that attacking players have on the ball. Sevens rugby is all about recognising space and beating the opposition. It places a huge amount of emphasis on running rugby and scoring tries. Players learn how to beat opposition in one-on-one or even two-on-one scenarios and this vital skill, as well as many more, can be carried over to the full fifteen-a-side game. The fitness levels required to play the game are immense. By not competing, Ireland is missing out.

The 2013 Rugby World Cup Sevens took place in Moscow during the last weekend in June. The men's tournament comprised twenty-four teams, including New Zealand, the eventual champions, and England, the beaten finalists. Nearly all of the top-tier IRB nations took part, along with the likes of Kenya, Spain, Georgia, Uruguay, Japan and Zimbabwe. Of the Six Nations Championship teams, Ireland and Italy were the only two not represented. Wales reached the quarter-finals before being beaten by New Zealand, while Scotland lost in the plate semi-final to Canada.

The greatest sevens player – Fiji's Waisale Serevi has time to showboat before touching down for a try.

If Wales and Scotland can field a team on the sevens circuit, why can't Ireland? The last time the IRFU had representation at an IRB Sevens event was at the World Cup back in 2009. Since then, the governing body has pleaded poverty as the main reason not to enter a team. Instead, the union has focused its efforts on promoting the Irish Wolfhounds or the Ireland 'A' team in meaningless friendlies once or twice a year. Why not scrap the Wolfhounds altogether and concentrate resources into putting a sevens squad together?

The talent is certainly there. The provincial academies are bursting with young, supremely fit players who would benefit hugely from competing and training regularly in a sevens environment. As it stands, the system in the senior game means that young players coming out of the Under-20s setup remain largely unused and unexposed in their respective squads.

Unless a twenty-one-year-old is exceptionally talented (exceptions to the rule are rare enough), they are left to compete in the British and Irish Cup or 'A' interprovincials throughout the season. Two or three years playing in an international sevens circuit developing their skills would do the majority of those young players the world of good.

England, Wales and Scotland all currently use their sevens squad to develop and bring through young talent. If you look at the 2013 Lions squad that travelled to Australia under Warren Gatland, Justin Tipuric, George North and Alex Cuthbert had all come through the Wales sevens programme. There are many more players in the England, Scotland and Wales senior squads with a sevens backgrounds on their CV.

Internationally, the list of former sevens players that have gone to greater things in the fifteen-a-side game reads like a who's who of international rugby stars – Israel Dagg, Cory Jane, Joe Rokocoko, Doug Howlett, J.P. Pietersen, Bryan Habana, Sireli Bobo, Matt Dawson, Mils Muliaina, Lote Tuqiri, Taku Ngwenya, Adam Thomson ... I could go on. These superstars all cut their cloth on the sevens circuit and used the skills learned there to further their rugby careers.

The revenue potential that would come with an Ireland sevens team is obvious. The IRFU would have little difficulty in securing a sponsor that would contribute to, or even cover the cost of, sending a squad out to compete on the circuit. Hosting a sevens event in Dublin would be a no-brainer. Imagine thousands of fans descending on the city for a weekend of international sevens rugby at the Aviva Stadium? Exactly.

Ireland has yet to experience the kind of mass player exodus currently affecting New Zealand, Fiji and South Africa but given there are only four professional teams operating here, I feel it's only a matter of time before the up-and-coming talent gets restless for first-team action. It would be a terrible waste of resources to invest in training and developing the next generation of players only to see them leave for overseas clubs because they cannot get sufficient game time in Ireland.

A sevens squad would provide an opportunity for some of those guys to travel the world and learn new skills that would benefit them further on in their careers. The clock is ticking. This needs to happen now.

4 GREAT HALF-BACK COMBINATIONS

1. John O'Meara and Jack Kyle

This partnership played together just eighteen times in the 1950s, but it was the iconic pairing of the period. Legions of schoolboys imitated the radio commentators, 'O'Meara to Kyle going left.' It is important to remember when considering this pairing that the ball of the period was the old leather Gilbert, which, when wet, was incredibly difficult to pass or kick. To move the ball quickly, the scrum-half had to dive pass and below is a wonderful photograph of O'Meara, horizontal with his feet off the ground, delivering a pass to Kyle. The offside law at the time put the defenders immeasurably closer, so speed of pass was vital and O'Meara gave Kyle space.

2. Colin Patterson and Ollie Campbell

Patterson partnered Tony Ward five times and Campbell six. However, it was with Campbell that we saw the flowering of the relationship that might have made a huge difference to Irish rugby had Patterson's career not been ended so tragically early by injury. Campbell's career may also have suffered as a result of the injury to the scrum-half. The failed experiment of using the out-half in the centre might never have happened if the Irish selectors had had two attacking half-backs at their disposal. In the 1979 Five Nations, the Irish back division scored five tries, three of them by Patterson. For a short period, Ireland had a fast passer, a devastating breaker and a threat to back-row forwards at number nine. We saw all too little of them together.

3. Peter Stringer and Ronan O'Gara

Backlines in rugby require time and space – the great half-backs provide both. Stringer is probably the best passer we have ever seen at number nine for Ireland and it begs the question why schools coaching in Ireland has not produced others to his standard. Stringer rarely broke, and kicked to an average standard, which prompted the criticism that he placed too much pressure on O'Gara because the defenders knew that he would pass. However, such was the speed of his pass and the telepathy between the pair that O'Gara was rarely under pressure from defenders.

4. John Robbie and Ollie Campbell

After making their debut together, this duo did not play again as a partnership for five years. The reputation of the pairing is based on their performances for Leinster. Campbell was the attacking mastermind and Robbie, the captain, the decision-maker and the loyal inside man. Incredibly, Robbie never played on a winning Irish team nor did he, as one of the great leaders of his era, captain an Irish side. Campbell was unlucky that two of the best scrum-halves in Ireland had truncated relationships with him.

RUGBY
2007
WORLD CUP

The 2007 Rugby World Cup in France was the scene of Irish rugby's most bitter disappointment. Coach Eddie O'Sullivan had at his disposal the most talented and exciting bunch of footballers this country has ever known, but, rather than deliver what should have been a record-breaking campaign, Ireland were sent packing at the conclusion of the pool stages.

Ireland's premature exit in France remains a mystery to this day. Players in that squad, now since retired, still struggle to put their finger on where it all went wrong. There has been a litany of excuses offered from everyone with an opinion on the game, but the facts of the case all point to a head coach who got his preparation and tactics hopelessly wrong.

Ireland played three warm-up matches going into their opening pool game against Namibia: a narrow win over Italy at Ravenhill, a 31–21 defeat to Scotland followed by a shambolic performance against the French club Bayonne, which almost cost Brian O'Driscoll his place in the tournament. O'Sullivan, who publicly prided himself on his organisational skills, made the bizarre decision to send his team out against a French club side less than four weeks before Ireland were due to play France in the pool stage of the World Cup. Is it any surprise that Ireland's best player was targeted? Luckily for O'Driscoll and his coach, the Ireland captain managed to recover from a horrific eye injury in time to play in the opening game.

'Hope is a dangerous thing, hope can drive a man insane.'

Morgan Freeman's famous line in *The Shawshank Redemption* epitomises perfectly why the country mourned Ireland's early exit in France. Expectations were at fever pitch going into the tournament; Irish fans were confident of reaching the semi-finals for the first time. All the ingredients were there. O'Sullivan had the players and the right form to deliver a masterpiece – but somewhere along the way, the chef spoiled the broth.

My own memories of that tournament stand out for a few different reasons. RTÉ Sport had no TV presence during the tournament, having lost the rights to Setanta and TV3, but with Newstalk securing the radio rights, I travelled over for the opening match between France and Argentina with Hugh Cahill as part of Newstalk's commentary team.

The French turned out in their thousands at the Stade de France to watch what they had hoped would be the start of a memorable tournament on home soil. Argentina, however, had different ideas. The South Americans shocked the rugby world with a 17–12 victory over Les Bleus in Saint Denis and the Pumas celebrated like they had won the tournament. The French were left gobsmacked and angry, and there were immediate calls for Bernard Laporte's head to be strapped to a guillotine. As Hugh and I boarded the train

BOD – no man has given more of his body for his country.

Eddie O'Sullivan – history will be kinder to his achievements.

to Bordeaux the following day, we wondered if the Pumas' victory over France was a sign of things to come. We did not have to wait long for an answer.

Ireland's opening match against Namibia in Bordeaux should have sent alarm bells ringing that something wasn't right in the camp. The cream of Irish professional rugby struggled to see off a side that mostly comprised amateur players and ranked twenty-second – fifteen places below Ireland – in the IRB standings. Brian O'Driscoll's brilliant solo try saved Ireland's blushes and O'Sullivan's charges limped over the line to win 32–17. It was far from convincing.

The Stade Chaban-Delmas also played host to Ireland's second pool match against Georgia. If Namibia was a bad start, Georgia was a complete and utter disaster. Ireland got bullied and bossed around the pitch for eighty long minutes by a tougher, stronger and more physical Georgia pack and, but for some heroic defending in the final few minutes, Ireland could easily have lost the game. A 14–10 win did little to ease the pressure that was beginning to mount on the team and the coach.

Throughout the tournament, the Ireland squad was locked away and out of sight. Players complained openly of boredom and fatigue after being forced to undergo gruelling training sessions in the build-up to matches. Irish newspapers carried photos of the players walking around the team hotel, muscle bound and bursting out of their T-shirts. They certainly looked in great shape, but they didn't play like it.

As the penultimate game against France approached, nerves began to filter through. France already had one defeat – if they suffered another, they were finished. But it was Ireland that played poorly from start to finish. O'Sullivan's side seemed nervous and lethargic as they had done in the opening two games and they never looked even remotely like troubling their opposition. France won comfortably, 25–3.

The writing was on the wall before Ireland took to the field for their must-win game against Argentina. A team that had failed to show anything near its best form in the first three rounds once again failed to gel, and the Pumas sealed their place in the quarter-finals with a 30–15 victory. Ireland were out of the World Cup and an entire country was left scratching its head.

So what went wrong? There have been many theories offered on the causes of Ireland's disaster in France, but if you examine the Irish structure in the build-up to the tournament, it isn't difficult to see what happened. O'Sullivan's dictatorial style of coaching left very little room for manoeuvre. Each player in his first-choice fifteen was assured of his position, regardless of performance. There was no competition for places and the players outside O'Sullivan's circle of trust understood that their role was insignificant. It didn't matter what happened on the pitch or how the players went in training, the first-choice starters were guaranteed their positions.

This is a recipe for disaster in any squad. If the front fifteen felt no pressure to perform, how could they be expected to compete with the best in the world? O'Sullivan refused to take any blame for what happened in France and he continued in the job for another Six Nations campaign. But the disappointment of the World Cup campaign hung over the remainder of his time with Ireland like a heavy black shadow. Even now, it is incomprehensible to me that an Ireland squad with that amount of talent could perform so abjectly.

Ronan O'Gara V Jonathan Sexton

We covet what we see every day.

Ambition allows for respect, but it has no room for friendship – particularly on the rugby field. With so much on the line, top dog takes all. In a small pool, second best isn't worth the silver it's printed on.

They were rivals and it could never have been any other way. If Jonathan Sexton was to establish himself as Ireland's first-choice fly-half, he would have to usurp the man who had dominated the number ten jersey in both green and red for the best part of a decade.

Sexton grew up watching Ronan O'Gara. He could only have admired a man who oozed confidence and calm in equal measure. O'Gara's qualities at fly-half were obvious from early in his career, but the Cork Con clubman had to battle hard for every inch of his success. O'Gara was never the quickest or the strongest player but what he lacked in stature and pace, he more than made up for in self-belief. O'Gara demanded attention because he believed more than anybody else that he was good enough to make it. And make it he did. But his journey wasn't easy. He practised and scrapped for every morsel of success and when Sexton came sniffing around his patch, he wasn't about to let this bright young thing take his crown without a fight.

That their paths would eventually cross wasn't always inevitable. Just as O'Gara struggled to escape the shadows of other fly-halves in his early years, Sexton's career almost never got going. But for an injury to Felipe Contepomi in one of the biggest games in Irish rugby history, Sexton's time might never have come.

With Leinster battling for supremacy against their archrivals Munster in the semi-final of the 2009 Heineken Cup, Sexton entered the arena at Croke Park to a cauldron of hostility and tension. His very first act required him to kick a penalty and push Leinster ahead.

Sexton placed the ball on the hallowed GAA turf, took a deep breath and calmly slotted the three points. I watched him that afternoon, wondering how he might handle his nerves. His performance in helping Leinster reach the final that year marked a turning point in his career. He took his chance with both hands.

One moment stands out from that match. When Gordon D'Arcy crossed for a Leinster try midway through the first half, Sexton ran over to O'Gara and roared triumphantly in his opponent's face. It was a stupid thing to do given that the match was far from over, but it revealed a burning desire in the St Mary's man. He was setting out his stall. Sexton desperately wanted what O'Gara closely protected. That moment marked the beginning of a rivalry that would continue for almost four years.

O'Gara was never going to roll over and play dead. Nothing in his history or personality would allow him to hand over a jersey he had worked so hard to attain. Blood, sweat and tears had gone in to preserving the number ten on his back for Munster and Ireland and when a rival emerged to challenge his position, O'Gara had to dig in and fight.

Both men travelled with the Ireland squad to the 2011 World Cup in New Zealand, vying for the fly-half jersey. Sexton's form for Leinster had been outstanding, his goal-kicking and attacking style contributing significantly to the province's two Heineken Cup titles. O'Gara could only watch as Munster struggled to find form while his international rival enjoyed universal acclaim. It can't have been easy. Both men arrived in New Zealand expecting to start the opening game against the USA. Declan Kidney went with Sexton. O'Gara, ever the warrior, must have found it difficult to take.

That campaign defined the changing of the guard. Sexton went from competing with his rival to usurping his role in the Ireland starting fifteen. When Sexton was named in the side to play Australia in the second pool game at Eden Park, O'Gara's international obituary was written. Even then, when the Munster man came on to close out the game midway through the second half with two penalties of his own, O'Gara was mentally spent.

In his post-match interview, his emotions got the better of him and you could see the acceptance on his face. His time with Ireland was coming to an end and while there would be other days, they would be few and far between.

It is unfair to compare these two great men because their paths crossed at different stages. O'Gara was in the final years of his professional career when Sexton came knocking and the Cork Con fly-half had overseen so many glorious days in green throughout his career. His poise and precision won Ireland a Grand Slam. Countless times, he kicked his country to victory – he never wavered and seldom faltered.

Now, Sexton reigns supreme. The day will come when he too will be challenged for the Ireland jersey. Just as it did for O'Gara and David Humphreys before him and many more before him. Rivalries are born out of passion and two more passionate rugby men you would struggle to find.

10 GREAT IRISH FLY-HALVES

1. Jack Kyle

Kyle has had no peer as fly-half for Ireland.

2. Mike Gibson

Gibson made his debut at Twickenham in 1964, where he was part of that famous criss-cross try by Pat Casey. It is a testament to his extraordinary ability that, despite winning sixty-nine caps for Ireland, he only made twenty-five appearances at fly-half and yet, on the basis of that small number of games, I have ranked him as the second-best Irish number ten of all time. Gibson had all the skills to reach the top, but he also had a tremendous work ethic in training. Former Irish fly-half Mick Quinn tells the story of going to meet him in Belfast to talk about playing for Ireland and he trained

with the Ulsterman for an afternoon. In those simple amateur days, Gibson's training regime was not equalled, and wouldn't be until the game went professional. His extraordinary commitment to physical conditioning meant that he played rugby until he was forty. Gibson had very high standards, which is why he probably really reached the peak of his career when he played at centre outside Barry John on the 1971 Lions tour to New Zealand. The bigger the stage, the better Gibson played. His move to centre was unlikely, and only came about when he missed the France game through injury in 1969 and was replaced by Barry McGann. Such was McGann's performance that the selectors decided to stay with the Cork Constitution man and move Gibson to centre for the England game and so began a new career.

3. Ollie Campbell

Campbell had an unfortunate start to his international career. With John Robbie at scrum-half, the duo had been outstanding for Leinster and were selected together for their debuts against Australia at Lansdowne Road in 1976. Ireland were beaten 20–10 – the fly-half was dropped and the scrum-half got just one more chance a few weeks

The metronomic Campbell kicks another goal.

later against France. Ireland were to play eighteen games before Campbell donned the green shirt again, and then he did so in controversial circumstances. Ireland toured Australia in the summer of 1979 and Tony Ward was the man in possession, with a huge reputation across Europe. To everybody's surprise, including Ward himself, Campbell was chosen for the test matches. Ireland won both and the Old Belvedere number ten went on to play twenty-two times for Ireland, scoring 217 points.

His stellar career lasted just four seasons but, in that time, he demonstrated what a great player he was for Ireland and the Lions. He was unlucky in that, although he toured twice for the Lions to South Africa and New Zealand, they were largely unsuccessful tours and he was never seen at his best. His greatest triumph was in 1982 when Ireland won the Triple Crown under Ciaran Fitzgerald. Campbell masterminded victory against Wales, kicked the vital conversion against England from the touchline and scored all the points against Scotland in the defining game at Lansdowne Road. His practice routines were legendary, and after the momentous victory over England at Twickenham, he went straight from the airport on the Sunday to Anglesea Road for kicking practice. However, he was much more than a kicker. He was unutterably brave as a defender and a strong passer out of both hands. In fact, he often commented that he had done so much practice with his weak left hand that it became his strength. And, of course, at a time when many fly-halves were standing deep, Campbell developed what is now standard practice – to stand flat and attack the advantage line.

4. Ronan O'Gara

O'Gara first crossed my radar when Eddie O'Sullivan and I were coaching in the USA and heard of a young man at Cork Constitution who had been born in San Diego. He was not at that point in the Munster squad and we tried to persuade him without success to declare for the American Eagles. I next saw him play for Cork Constitution against Lansdowne in an AIL game when he was still a mere club player. I was covering the match for the *Irish Independent* and, the following day, wrote: 'O'Gara attacks the advantage line better than any Irish fly-half I have seen since Ollie Campbell.' O'Gara duly played for Munster and Ireland and is the record points-scorer for every team on which he has played and in every competition in which he has played. As a tactical kicker, he was without parallel in world rugby, he passed superbly off either hand and he had nerves of steel when it came to taking crucial penalty kicks or drop goals. He certainly wasn't a frontline defender, but nobody could ever have questioned his courage.

5. Barry McGann

One wonders how good McGann might have been had he played in the professional era. He was the most unlikely looking fly-half, even at a time when international players trained just twice a week. His rotund figure disguised one of the shrewdest brains in rugby and his tactical kicking was straight out of the Cork and Munster handbook. He kicked with a short backswing, but with immense power; no doubt a product of his soccer skills which had seen him earn international honours as a schoolboy and play League of Ireland football at Shelbourne. It was an indication of his class that Ireland were prepared to move the incomparable Mike Gibson to centre to accommodate the young Corkman, who won twenty-five caps in six seasons. His last match was against New Zealand in Wellington in 1976 after which, in a quirk of fate, he was replaced by Gibson for the following year's Five Nations.

6. Jonathan Sexton

Sexton's seemingly lowly position in sixth place is partially due to the fact that his career is not over and therefore is difficult to assess. To date, he has had some astonishing success, but there are question marks about his ability to manage a game and to close out victories in the final stages. His great strengths are his ebullient confidence, his aggressive defence and his complete comfort with ball in hand. Like O'Gara, he is a nerveless place-kicker. A Lions selection and now one of the highest paid rugby players in France are clear indications of his worth.

7. Paul Dean

Dean was the outstanding schoolboy of his generation. Even at a young age, he demonstrated handling skills that were way above the ordinary. He came to St Mary's RFC straight from school and, though the club resisted the temptation to push him into the first team too quickly, there was no stopping the young man once he'd played at senior level.

Dean's big drawback as a number ten was that he was a very poor kicker of the ball, tactically and for touch. He was first capped for Ireland on the South African tour of 1981, where his kicking let him down and he was moved to the centre for the

second test. He won his next five caps in the centre before spending two years in the wilderness. He was famously brought back, by new coach Mick Doyle, against Australia in 1984. A non-kicking fly-half seemed to fit in with Doyle's 'give it a lash' philosophy. It was the most fruitful period in Dean's career, when he was an integral part of the Triple Crown-winning side. Three-quarters loved playing outside Dean, whose fast hands give them time and space.

8. David Humphreys

It is hard to know why Humphreys ranks so low in my pantheon of great fly-halves. After all, at the time of his retirement, he was Ireland's most-capped player in that position, having played seventy-two times and scored 560 points. He had a marvellous armoury for the pivotal position in rugby. He kicked superbly from the hand and from the ground with a particular penchant for drop goals.

He was devastatingly quick off the mark and some of his breaks, particularly in Ulster's march to a Heineken Cup victory in 1999, were quite outstanding. His weakness, like O'Gara, his great competitor for the number ten shirt at Ireland, was his poor defence. Ulster with Andy Ward on the flank did a better job of protecting him than the flankers at Ireland. He was also never fully appreciated as a captain outside his native province.

9. Tony Ward

Ward has excited more debate in Irish rugby than perhaps any other player of his generation. The question was whether he or Campbell should be the Irish fly-half. To this very day, trenchant positions are taken up whenever that period in Irish rugby is discussed. Famously, the Irish selectors tried to play both players in the same backline, moving Campbell to centre, but it was never a success. Ward always reminded me of when a slimline Barry McGann was a soccer player. Ward could put the ball on a sixpence with the boot but, unlike McGann, was less good at assessing space and was an average passer. He did however possess a searing break and sidestep which confused the opposition, but sometimes made him a difficult player to connect with for the next pass.

He came to the Irish team at an important juncture when he was capped against Scotland in the first match of the 1978 Five Nations Championship. Ireland were coming off two seasons with just one victory and Ward's tactical kicking, and particularly his superb place-kicking, were crucially important in giving the side a new confidence – although the results in his nine matches at number ten were not markedly better than those before he was playing.

He was then famously dropped in Australia and his career never reached the same heights in his subsequent appearances for Ireland – perhaps his finest ever performance was in Thomond Park in 1978 when he was outstanding in Munster's historic victory over the All Blacks.

10. Mick English

It is an indication of the talent of the players who've played at fly-half for Ireland that Mick English of Munster, Ireland and the Lions can only get in at number ten on this list. He was a quintessential Munster fly-half – he had a kick like a mule, could execute Garryowens and drop goals with equal facility, and was a tough tackler in defence. English was part of the 1959 Lions tour to Australia and New Zealand but, sadly, was injured early on and had to return home. Given the outstanding back play on that tour, it would have been interesting to see how he would have performed in the different environment.

His first cap against Wales in 1958 came after the retirement of the legendary Jack Kyle, a hard act to follow. English did remarkably well in his next six tests, which led to his Lions selection. Astonishingly, he was replaced by six fly-halves in his career before finally giving way to Mike Gibson. In an indication of the selection policies of the time, English discovered that he had lost his place on the Irish team when hearing the announcement on the radio.

If only they had played in another position

Somebody once said that there was no shortage of talent in Irish rugby, but there was a massive shortage of talent that can recognise talent. All too often players are given a role because of their size, their weight or their speed – or lack of it. Thus small, quick players become backs and big, slow players become forwards. However, the game is changing fast. Players are now bigger and stronger than ever and many backs in the modern game are taller and heavier than second rows of the amateur era.

So, I've taken a look at players who might have had more success if they had played in a position other than the one they were first handed.

1. Shane Jennings

He should have fifty caps. He has spent most of his career playing at a time when Ireland has been without a specialist open-side flanker. Jennings has always been a number seven by choice and mindset. Sadly, he has not been good enough to nail down a regular place. Yet he has pace, possesses good hands, and is eminently brave, tough and abrasive. If only somebody had looked at him at age fourteen and said, 'Jennings, you are a hooker', then he might have

spent his summer with the Lions in Australia. Sadly in schools, there are too many short little fat boys who have to be accommodated in the front row and not enough quick, skilful ones to play in the back row. The schools' gain is Ireland's loss.

2. David Quinlan and James Downey

Two players who have played at inside centre with limited success. Quinlan, now retired, won two caps for Ireland and, of course, Downey continues to perform for Munster. Interestingly, they are almost the exact same height and weight, tipping the scales at 104 kilograms and standing six foot four inches tall. By the standards of top-level rugby, they could not be described as quick, thus their carers condemned them to being crash-ball carriers and strong defenders at inside centre. Imagine then what might have happened if an imaginative coach at schoolboy level had taken them aside and turned them into blindside flankers. Slow centres would be very quick flankers, average passers in midfield, would be outstanding handlers as back rows and crash-ball merchants at inside centre, would probably top the ball-carrying statistics in the back row. The tragedy for Quinlan and Downey is that very often in schools rugby size has a disproportionate effect, and these players who would have had stellar schoolboy careers were never likely to make it at the top level. Definitely two that got away.

3. Stephen Ferris

This man is an unlikely candidate for playing out of position. However, Ireland's rugby history is littered with a large number of back-row forwards and a limited supply of world-class second rows. 'World class' is the operative adjective here. Donncha O'Callaghan for all his commitment and effort and a Lions tour selection has never set the world on fire as a ball carrier. Recent years have shown that one of the biggest problems facing the Irish team is a shortage of ball carriers. Ferris, in his truncated career, has demonstrated that quality and a move to the second row would have made space in the back row where

Stephen Ferris – the epitome of toughness.

there are candidates aplenty. Because of the injuries that have dogged his career, it is difficult to quantify just how good he really could have been. But I for one would have loved to have seen him in a rampaging partnership with Paul O'Connell.

4. Brian O'Driscoll

Now here's a surprising choice for a change of jersey number. Why would the greatest centre in Irish rugby history be considered for another position? The answer is because even though he is the greatest, would he have been even greater in another position? Open-side flankers are a particular breed and that is why they are so rare. The great Irish teams were founded on outstanding number sevens. The 1948 Grand Slam had Jim McCarthy, the 1982 Triple Crown had the wonderful Fergus Slattery and Ciaran Fitzgerald led Ireland to another Triple Crown with Nigel Carr on the flank. There has never been a better three-quarter on the ground than O'Driscoll. Time out of number he wins ball at rucks by dint of his low centre of gravity and powerful upper body strength. He is a devastating tackler and possesses the priceless asset of acceleration over ten yards. If O'Driscoll had played at number seven, he would have made Jean Pierre Rives look average. Sadly, I will only see it in my dreams.

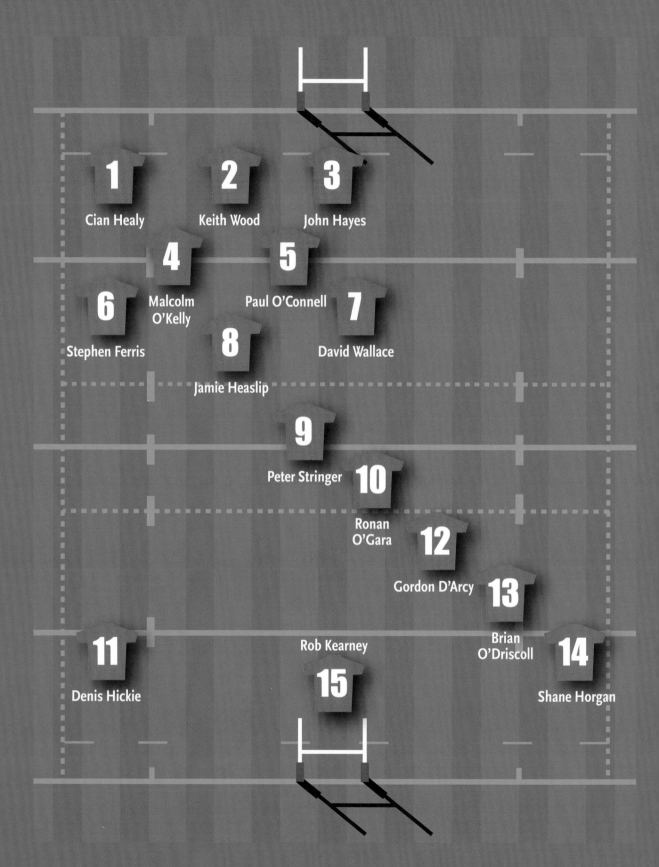

MY GREATEST IRISH TEAM 1999–PRESENT

 Rob Kearney

Girvan Dempsey and Geordan Murphy might feel hard done by here but, for me, Kearney's talent and skill in a most difficult position make him stand apart. His athleticism and fearlessness under the high ball almost defies physics, a testament to his early days on the Gaelic football field. Kearney is rock solid in defence and his attacking game has grown in tandem with his confidence and belief in himself over the years. His personality oozes with a quiet determination and he is both intelligent and insightful at full-back. His performances on the 2009 Lions tour to South Africa left many of those watching gobsmacked, as he consistently defied gravity and fear to dominate ball in the air. Still young, there is plenty more to come from the former Clongowes Wood star.

Honourable mentions: Geordan Murphy, Girvan Dempsey

 Gordon D'Arcy and Brian O'Driscoll

The selection of Gordon D'Arcy and Brian O'Driscoll will cause the least debate. If Declan Kidney is reading this, he might plump for Paddy Wallace at inside centre but, Deccie aside, I imagine we are all in agreement. These two players have provided the spine of the Irish backline for the past ten years. As a partnership, they surpassed Will Carling and Jeremy Guscott's world record for a centre combination when they played at the 2011 World Cup. Their time together for Leinster and Ireland enabled them to develop an understanding of each other's game based on friendship, mutual respect and gut instinct. Neither is the biggest man, but they were ferocious in defence and trusted each other to protect the centre as if their lives depended on it. D'Arcy and O'Driscoll were terrier-like in their approach to the breakdown. Each had mastered the art of stealing opposition ball off the deck and their strength and aggression in this area was without equal anywhere in the world. In attack, they were also clinical. O'Driscoll's try-scoring record speaks for itself, but I'm sure he would attest to the work that his centre partner put in to give him the space to operate so effectively. Ireland's greatest centre combination? It's hard to argue against.

Honourable mention: Kevin Maggs

Denis Hickie and Shane Horgan

The flying Leinster men. Hickie's pace marked him out as a threat from any area of the pitch, while Horgan's physical strength and ability to read the game was unparalleled. Together, they formed a lethal duo, each complementing the other's skill set perfectly. 2006 produced two incredible scores, one from each winger, that will be forever ingrained in my memory.

Horgan's try against England at Twickenham to win the Triple Crown epitomises what he brought to the Ireland jersey. The Meath man had no right to force his way over in the corner but somehow he managed to use his six-foot-four frame to hold off the tackle of Lewis Moody and reach for the line to score his sixteenth international try and win the game for Ireland. It was an incredible feat of balance, strength and skill.

Hickie scored some memorable tries for club and country over his eleven-year career, but it was that magical year again, 2006, that springs to mind. Leinster travelled to the Stadium Municipal to play the mighty Toulouse in the quarter-final of the Heineken Cup. It was an enthralling contest from start to finish, best encapsulated by Hickie's incredible try in the second half. Leinster turned the ball over deep in their own twenty-two and charged into a counter-attack. Felipe Contepomi spotted Hickie in space on the left wing and set him free with a beautifully floated pass. Hickie sprinted up the field, exchanging passes with Gordon D'Arcy, before backing himself to touch down in the corner to eruptions among the travelling support. Leinster won that quarter-final against all the odds, before Munster taught them a valuable lesson in the semi-final weeks later at Lansdowne Road. Between them, Denis Hickie and Shane Horgan scored fifty tries for Ireland during their international careers and both played significant roles in the success enjoyed by Ireland and Leinster over the past fifteen years.

Honourable mentions: Tommy Bowe, Luke Fitzgerald

10 Ronan O'Gara

The exclusion of Jonathan Sexton at fly-half is bound to ruffle a few feathers. Sexton is the in-form number ten in Irish rugby, but with 126 caps for Ireland and over 1,000 international points, Ronan O'Gara is my only choice at this position. His partnership with Peter Stringer, forged in their schooldays together at Pres Cork, is one of the most enduring in the game. O'Gara is one of the most intelligent fly-halves I have ever seen and his ability to read the game and put the ball on a sixpence kept his career going well into his thirties. He will forever be a part of Munster history with two Heineken Cup medals and his partnership with Stringer must be the longest in the professional game.

Honourable mentions: Jonny Sexton, David Humphreys

9 Peter Stringer

Peter Stringer proved that a large frame was not a prerequisite for playing rugby at the highest level. He remains one of the best passers of a ball in the world and his ability to take down men four times his size continues to whip crowds into a frenzy.

Honourable mention: Conor Murphy

8 Jamie Heaslip

Jamie Heaslip edges out Anthony Foley and Victor Costello for the number eight jersey. An underage star in the 2004 Under-20 World Cup in Scotland, Heaslip has gone on to be one of the most respected number eights in the game. He has consistently defied the odds by dominating bigger and stronger opponents and it is to his enormous credit that he has remained injury-free for the majority of his career.

Honourable mentions: Anthony Foley, Victor Costello

7 David Wallace

The number seven jersey was a tight battle between two players. David Wallace and Keith Gleeson shared open-side international duties between them for much of the past twelve years, but David Wallace just edged him out of my selection. With over 200 appearances for Munster, seventy-two for Ireland and three for the Lions, Wallace was one of the outstanding players of the professional era. He had all the skills necessary to play in the back row and his versatility to slot in at number six, seven or eight made him worth his weight in gold for club and country. Wallace had incredible pace for such a big man. His ability to carry the ball and get over the gain line, even under pressure, provided many a platform for Munster and Ireland to go forward and make ground. His work in defence was equally impressive and his fitness levels were unparalleled in the game.

Honourable mention: Keith Gleeson

6 Stephen Ferris

Ireland's back row has been a source of argument and debate among many modern-day rugby fans. Each position carries with it different responsibilities and players are favoured according to philosophies on how the game should be played. Some regard Sean O'Brien as the ultimate open-side flanker. Others think he is best served at number six or eight. There are those who feel David Wallace played his best ruby at the back of the scrum, while others saw him only as a seven. I have selected the back row on the merits of their individual strength. But together, they represent an impressive unit.

Stephen Ferris' career has been blighted by injury. His talent was obvious from a very young age but it must be acknowledged that his legacy in the Irish game will never be truly realised. I remember Paul O'Connell emerging from a weights session with the Ireland squad in 2006 and being amazed by Ferris' natural strength. Ferris was twenty years of age at the time. When fit, he is an unstoppable wrecking machine. One of Ireland's most effective ball carriers in recent years, his natural aggression and hunger for physical contact made him the ideal player at blindside flanker. Unfortunately, his long battles with injury have meant we will never know just how good he could have been.

Honourable mentions: Sean O'Brien, Alan Quinlan

5 Paul O'Connell

My locks cross the Munster–Leinster divide. Paul O'Connell's name has always been one of the first on the team sheet. His professional career is a testament to his discipline, hard work and determination. A talented young swimmer in his day, O'Connell had the height but not the natural bulk necessary to forge a career as an international lock. Countless hours in the weights room and a diet plan that would render most of us morbidly obese within a week helped to manufacture the giant we see on the field today. When O'Connell gets injured, his greatest fear is not gaining weight, it's losing it. His presence in the Munster team set the platform for victory in the 2006 and 2008 Heineken cups. Without him, Ireland and Munster lack vital strength and leadership up front. His return to the Munster fold for the 2013 Heineken Cup quarter-final against Harlequins at Twickenham Stoop was phenomenal to watch. He soared highest in the lineout, stealing Quins' ball and providing Munster with a platform to hassle and harry the English opposition. O'Connell was simply magnificent and he inspired Munster to victory.

Honourable mention: Donncha O'Callaghan

4 Malcolm O'Kelly

Malcolm O'Kelly was, at times, incredibly frustrating to watch. He is perhaps the most gifted second row ever to play for Leinster and Ireland. His ability in the lineout, in attack and defence, made him a prized asset for club and country, but he was so much more than just a lineout man. At six foot eight, his size alone struck fear into the opposition. Malcolm on his day was as ferocious a lock as I've ever seen, but his naturally gentle nature meant he couldn't always give coaches that mad-dog performance – it had to be drawn out of him. When it did come, though, O'Kelly was a force to be reckoned with. His large, awkward physique enabled him to frustrate the life out of opponents without fear of reprisal. Leinster missed him desperately when he retired. Import after import was brought in to fill the void that O'Kelly left behind and very few (Nathan Hines and Brad Thorn aside) managed to justify their place in his absence.

Honourable mention: Mick Galwey

3 John Hayes

The pillar of Irish rugby for over a decade. The truth of it is that were it not for John Hayes' freakish ability to endure and hold up a scrum, Ireland would not have won a third of their test victories over the past twelve years. Everybody loved the Bull and he demanded the respect of colleagues and opposition players. His six-foot-five-inch frame was wholly inappropriate for tight-head prop, but he somehow managed to forge a technique to hold off the biggest brutes in the game. His quiet and unassuming demeanour masked a ferocious dedication to his art. Millions of Irish fans shared his burden over the years as they watched him lock horns time and time again in the front row. I will always remember John Hayes as the man who single-handedly carried the Irish scrum for 101 international caps.

Honourable mention: Mike Ross

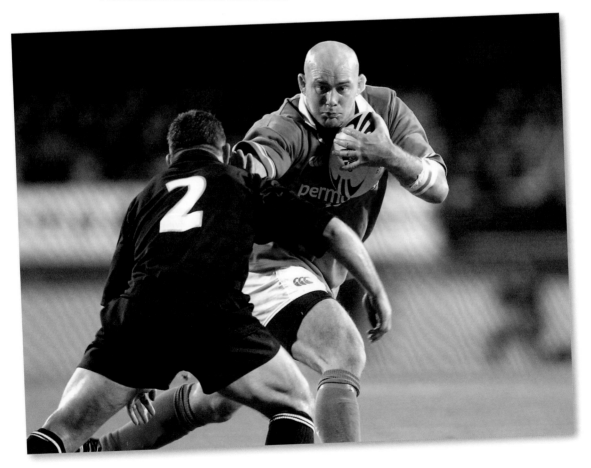

2 Keith Wood

There was no debate about who would be my hooker. Keith Wood was the first real superstar of Irish professional rugby. An ideal captain, he led his troops by example, tirelessly putting his body on the line. My fondest memory of Woody is of his famous try against England in the 2001 Six Nations Championship at Lansdowne Road. The foot-and-mouth crisis that year meant that the game was postponed until October. It was a big day for Woody as he eclipsed Tom Kiernan as Ireland's most capped skipper. And how he marked the occasion! A lineout throw to Mick Galwey on the English five-metre line made its way to Anthony Foley who popped the ball up beautifully to his captain on the burst. Woody was like a rabid dog smashing his way over Neil Back to touch down in front of a delirious home crowd. Ireland went on to win that match 20–14, and the captain's try became the symbol of that success. Woody was one of the first Irish players to carve out a professional career abroad. His decision to move to Harlequins broke many Munster hearts at the time, but such was his talent and reputation, he could have gone anywhere in the world and been a success.

Honourable mentions: Shane Byrne, Rory Best

1 Cian Healy

With thirty-five caps and at still only twenty-five years of age, Cian Healy is a shoe-in at loose-head. When you consider that prop-forwards generally don't mature until they reach their late twenties, it's almost frightening to ponder how good Healy could eventually become. His scrummaging ability has progressed on an upward curve over the past few years but it's not just his ability to pack down against the best in the world that sets him apart. His work rate and hunger in the loose wouldn't be out of place in a back-row forward. He actively seeks out the ball during play and screams to get on the end of passes. At six foot and eighteen-and-a-half stone, he is also phenomenally quick. His team-mates still marvel at his infectious enthusiasm for the game. I remember Jamie Heaslip remarking that Healy was the strongest human being he had ever met and Healy's record in the scrum, would appear to back that up.

Honourable mention: Marcus Horan, Reggie Corrigan

George's View

Should a try be worth six points?

In the sixth century BC, the Chinese general Sun Tzu declared, 'Invincibility lies in the defence; the possibility of victory in the attack.' On the other hand, the former Ireland coach Eddie O'Sullivan always believed that defence was easier than attack because it was not complicated by having possession of the ball.

To score a try in rugby union is immeasurably harder than completing a touchdown in American football or scoring a goal at soccer. Only in rugby does a player have to pass the ball backwards to go forwards. In rugby, unlike gridiron, there is no possibility of a quarter-back throwing the ball forty yards to a wide receiver. Similarly, unlike soccer, there is no opportunity for the midfielder to thread a pass through the defence for a forward to score.

In rugby a properly organised defence should always make it difficult for opponents to score. The game embodies the views of Sun Tzu in that, increasingly, professional teams are keeping clean sheets by making as many as 150 tackles in eighty minutes. In the modern era, prop-forwards make more tackles in a match than their amateur predecessors would have made in a lifetime.

The result is that the try is becoming increasingly rare and with goal-kickers now routinely having success rates of over 95 per cent, teams can concentrate on defence and wait for penalties to be awarded.

Since the modern scoring values were first adopted in 1948, they have been changed twice – on each occasion it was to increase the value of the try in the hope that this would encourage teams to attempt more expansive rugby.

The word 'try' comes from the rules agreed by the founding fathers of rugby. Touching the ball down gave the opportunity for the team to 'try' for a goal by kicking the ball over the bar. In 1875, it was decided that when teams were level on goals (or no goals had been scored), then the match would be decided by the number of tries. At that time, there was no point-scoring system as matches were simply decided by the number of goals.

Points were finally awarded in 1886 where a goal – i.e. a try and conversion – was worth three points and a try one point. At that point, there were no penalty goals although these, together with the mark and the other parts of the game we recognise today, were gradually introduced over the following years.

It was 1891 before an overall points system was adopted. The try and conversion was worth five points, but the three-point penalty goal was worth more than the two-point unconverted try. Interestingly, the kicking skill was deemed to be more valuable than the scoring of a try as the conversion and the penalty goal were worth three points.

Finally in 1905, the goal stayed at five points but the try was increased to three while the conversion was reduced to two. At this point, the drop goal was introduced and worth four points. One can only assume that because of the poor quality of the ball and Victorian attitudes to practice, which they deemed to be professional and thus working class, kicking was a rare skill and merited more points.

That system remained in place until 1948 when the drop goal was reduced to three points and, except for the amendments in 1971 which raised the try to four points and in 1992 to five points, it has been so for almost seventy years. The differential penalty or free kick from which no points could be scored was also introduced in the hope that it would reduce the reliance on kicking goals and tempt teams to go for a try.

However, today, despite the best efforts of the IRB, more games are decided by goal-kickers than by try-scorers. The improvement in the quality of the football and the kicking techniques of the players has made a penalty kick within fifty metres of the goalposts almost a formality.

Raising the value of the try to six points – or alternatively reducing the value of the penalty goal to two points – will not work. A change to the value of the try, given the rarity of the occurrence, will not be enough to guarantee victories. On the other hand, a reduction in the value of the penalty goal will simply mean that teams will consider it worthwhile to concede penalties rather than increase the possibility of a try. Thus, there cannot be a large gap in the value of tries versus penalty goals.

It is astonishing to think that the lawmakers of 150 years ago might well have had the right idea in awarding the game to the team that scored the most goals irrespective of the number of tries or penalty goals. It is unlikely that the IRB will return to that system, but something has to be done or tries will only be scored if there is a wide disparity in standard between the two teams.

The problem might best be solved by first enforcing the laws as they are written and secondly simplifying the incredibly complex interpretations at the scrum and the breakdown where the vast majority of penalties are awarded.

Rugby union is now a worldwide television spectacular and the broadcasters demand a game that can be understood by the uninitiated, is full of movement and has a high rate of physical collisions. American football fulfils all these conditions and rugby administrators are under pressure to provide that kind of game, particularly from unions in the southern hemisphere who face competition from other sports or are short of money.

If there were fewer opportunities to score points by kicking for goal, then the try – without any change in value – would become more important.

That could be done by reverting to the scrum patterns of fifty years ago, where the front rows made contact without the modern concept of the 'hit'. This would result in less resetting of the scrums and in turn fewer penalties. Today, in an effort to control the engagement, referees are routinely awarding a free kick at first scrum of the match irrespective of whether it is merited or not.

The result of this is that referees, to all intents and purposes, cannot with any certainty decide who is at fault. It is incredible that the lawmakers have decided that a penalty will be awarded if the front row goes up or goes down, when the laws of physics determine that if power comes on the point of contact, it must be released by an upward or downward motion.

The breakdown similarly is a mess and the game is not better now because one side can keep the ball through twenty phases or more. If the laws as written were effectively policed, there would be a penalty every time the ball carrier goes to ground.

American football creates a situation that if ten yards are not gained after four 'downs' then the ball is conceded to the other side. Similarly in rugby league, the side in possession loses the ball after the sixth tackle.

The answer for rugby union is not to raise the number of points awarded for a try but to create a set of laws that bring more and more forwards back into the ruck and out of the middle of the backline, where they simply clog up space to the advantage of the defenders and the disadvantage of attackers, thus making tries harder to score.

Changing the points value of the try will make no difference. What needs to be done is to create a game that enables tries to be scored and shifts the advantage to the attackers.

Hugh's View

Should a try be worth six points?

Goal-kickers are dominating rugby, a sport that has its roots and popularity in running and passing. It was never meant to be this way. Goal-kicking is the perfect accompaniment to this wonderful game but it has no business being centre stage, and something must be done to restore proper order on the pitch.

There is a premium on players who can banish their immediate surroundings, hold their nerve and slot kicks at goal under the most frenzied of pressure. Talented kickers spend hours and hours on training grounds all over the world, practising the art of kicking goals. It is indeed a fine art – but it's becoming too dominant a theme.

The emphasis on finding kicking machines like England's Jonny Wilkinson and Wales legend Neil Jenkins has reached crazy levels. Crazy, but justified under current laws. Place-kickers know their value and they are picked accordingly. If a coach has a choice between a brilliant all-round fly-half who can't kick goals and a sharpshooter with average running and tackling ability, he will choose the latter. This is mainly because the scoring system, as it stands, is biased towards kicking goals.

Why not make tries more appealing? If a try was worth six points, it would certainly alter team strategy during matches. As things stand, a good kicker has market value above and beyond any other individual talent. Why not change that? The emphasis needs to shift away from three-point exchanges and back on to the core values of the sport. Rugby is about running, passing and tackling. Kicking should be an afterthought.

There are two options here, as I see it. The IRB can either increase the value of a try from five to six points, or it can reduce the value of a kick at goal from three points to two. A two-

point margin, as is the case at the moment, is not sufficient to shift the emphasis away from penalty goals and onto scoring tries.

Let's look at an example:

Team A are trailing Team B by five points with eight minutes to go. They are awarded a penalty thirty-five metres out in front of the posts.

Under the current system, Team A would elect for a shot at goal and then play for a second penalty to win the game. But if a penalty goal were worth two points, Team A would need three shots at goal to win, so would more than likely elect to kick to touch and push for a try.

In an age when defences are so tight, we should be giving tries more reward.

People watch rugby to see tries. The more, the better. Either reduce the value of a kick at goal or increase the value of a try. Simple.

2011 RUGBY WORLD CUP

New Zealand – the home of rugby union? Based on the All Blacks' dominance on the pitch over the past twenty years, most would agree that it is. But for all of New Zealand's talent and history within the game, their record in world cups has been extremely poor. They tasted victory on home soil in 1987 and then nothing for twenty-four years. Every time the World Cup has come around, New Zealand has gone into the tournament as red-hot favourites – and each time, they have left empty handed. When the 2011 Rugby World Cup kicked off in Auckland, many wondered if the All Blacks' dreadful history with the Webb Ellis trophy would continue to haunt them. In truth, it very nearly did.

For the second time in eight years, Ireland had all the ingredients necessary to break their own dreadful record in the tournament and reach the semi-finals for the first time. Domestically, the Irish provinces were in rude health; Leinster had just won their second Heineken Cup title in three years and Ulster and Munster both had strong squads contributing to the national setup. Ireland had won the Six Nations Grand Slam just two years previously and despite some of the players' advancing years, the stage was set for these Irish players to show the world what they were capable of.

The structure of the tournament was such that Ireland's task was clearly set out before them. Declan Kidney had to negotiate his way past Australia and Italy in Pool B, to make it on to the weaker side of the draw for the quarter-finals. If Ireland topped the group, they would more than likely face Wales in the last eight, followed by France or England in the semi-final. But if Ireland finished second in the group, they faced a quarter-final with New Zealand.

There was massive pressure on the All Blacks from the very beginning. On the eve of the opening match against Tonga, the streets of Auckland were littered with posters of Richie McCaw, Dan Carter and Sonny Bill Williams. The expectation among the home support was overwhelming and, as kick-off in the opening game loomed, the pressure turned into tension. Everywhere you went, in the shops and bars, in every corner of both islands, it was all people talked about. New Zealanders didn't just hope for success in 2011, they absolutely demanded it.

But if Graham Henry's side felt any nerves in the curtain-raiser against the Pacific Islanders, they certainly didn't show it. The All Blacks demolished their opponents with some brilliant attacking flare, scoring tries for fun. It was a performance designed to lay down a marker to the rest of the teams – New Zealand, in their own country, were dead set on winning back the trophy that had eluded them for twenty-four long years.

While Tonga were chasing black shadows around Eden Park, Ireland were busy preparing for their opening game against the United States in New Plymouth. New Plymouth isn't what you would call the most scenic of spots. It didn't help matters that the weather was damp, grey and overcast, but the fans who had travelled to support the Irish team were in confident spirits. The Eagles, coached by Eddie O'Sullivan, weren't expected to pose many problems for an Ireland side that had undergone the perfect preparation in the beautiful surroundings of Queenstown. But the game did not go according to plan.

Declan Kidney surprised many by selecting twenty-one-year-old scrum-half Conor Murray for his first international start. It was a bold move, particularly given Eoin Reddan's impressive form for Leinster the previous season. Murray acquitted himself well in tough conditions but Ireland performed poorly and had to grind out a win in a dour spectacle of a game. Immediately Irish minds raced back to France and 2007 – was this poor start a sign of things to come? Kidney and the rest of the management group insisted all was well and that Ireland would be ready for the Australians in Eden Park in round two. The fans and the media made their way to Auckland more in hope than anticipation.

From the first minute against the Wallabies, Ireland unleashed hell. They hounded and savaged the shell-shocked Wallabies, never giving Robbie Deans' side an inch. Ireland's defence coach Les Kiss had set out a plan to dismantle the Australians' off-loading game by applying the choke tackle at every available opportunity. It worked brilliantly. Each time Quade Cooper or James O'Connor tried a little slip or flick to unlock the Irish defence, the choke tackle locked in tight to smother the man in possession and prevent the pass from going. It frustrated the Wallabies enormously, resulting in penalties for Ireland and points on the board. Mike Ross and Cian Healy were immense in the scrum, targeting the Wallaby front row with each hit and coming out on top in most of the exchanges. Donncha

O'Callaghan had one of the games of his life, bullying and bashing his way around the field like an angry pit bull. Deep into the second half, Tommy Bowe intercepted the ball inside the Irish twenty-two-metre line and sprinted the length of the field. An incredible last-ditch tackle from James O'Connor denied the Ulsterman a famous try but Ireland didn't need it. When the final whistle sounded, Ireland had beaten the Wallabies for the first time in a World Cup match. Eden Park exploded with green.

The Irish invasion of New Zealand only added to the buzz around the team camp. Thousands of young Irish fans in their twenties and early thirties flew in from Australia to support their heroes. Everywhere the team went, supporters followed. There were queues outside hotels where fans gathered, hoping to get their picture taken with the players. For many, this was a chance to reconnect with home. Some hadn't been back to Ireland in years. Now, Ireland had come to them.

The victory over Australia changed everything. Ireland had gone from World Cup by-the-ways to serious contenders in the space of eighty enthralling minutes. Comfortable wins over Russia and Italy followed and Ireland advanced to the quarter-finals of the tournament as pool winners. They were drawn to play the runners-up in Pool D – Wales. Ireland had had a strong record against the Welsh in recent years and players and supporters licked their lips at the prize on offer for seeing off their Celtic neighbours. Nobody could have foreseen what would happen next.

The defeat to Wales in the quarter-final has probably been the most difficult Irish result to stomach for many years. Few outside of Wales thought Ireland could lose that match. Spirits in the camp were high, results had gone their way and the performances up to then had been as good as could have been expected. The players had come through the pool phase relatively unscathed and everything was set up for Ireland to go on and reach the semi-finals. But, for whatever reason, it just didn't happen.

Wales, as we would subsequently learn, had been steadily building throughout that competition. Warren Garland had at his disposal a young, extremely fit and hungry bunch of players and Ireland were completely taken by surprise. Wales' intensity from the off caught Ireland asleep and by the time Declan Kidney's side realised what was happening, it was all over. Ireland, shell-shocked and bemused, trudged off the pitch as losing quarter-finalists yet again.

There are a few reasons why I feel we lost that match. Kidney, until his dying breath, will never admit to underestimating Wales but everything about the Irish performance that day suggests the players expected to win before they ever set foot on the field. Contrast that game with Ireland's performance against Australia. In Eden Park, we were first to everything and refused to give an inch. In Wellington, we simply did not turn up. Wales, led by the phenomenal Sam Warburton, stalked Ireland all around the pitch. Gatland completely out-smarted his opposite number and for all the Irish talk about finally reaching the last four, we forgot about getting the job done in the quarter-finals.

As many had predicted, New Zealand did go on to claim glory on home soil. The All Blacks were certainly the best side in the tournament overall, but they were not the best team in the final. An appalling display of refereeing by South African Craig Joubert robbed France of the title. Marc Lièvremont's unlikely run to the final was almost the story of the tournament. The French had been plagued by in-fighting and tactical madness by the head coach and very few, including their own press, gave them any chance of success. Somehow they managed to scrap their way to the final in Auckland and but for two astonishing decisions by Joubert in the closing stages where France should have been awarded kickable penalties, Les Bleus would have spoiled the All Backs' party. But New Zealand clung on for dear life and the relief, more than joy, on the faces of players, coaches and supporters at the final whistle was palpable. The All Blacks finally had their trophy back.

In a game often played with intense physicality, the lightest of touches can sometimes make all the difference.

3 GREAT RUGBY GROUNDS

1. The Mardyke Grounds, Cork

To everybody in Cork, it is known as 'the Dyke'. It is now part of University College Cork's sports complex, but for my entire school-going life, it was the major ground in the city where all the big soccer and rugby matches were played.

On Saturdays, it hosted club rugby games and on Sundays, or at least alternate Sundays, it was the home ground of the Cork soccer team. And of course on Wednesday afternoons, it hosted schools cup matches. There are only two rugby schools in Cork –

The Mardyke was a ground where the crowd could almost be part of the action.

the fee-paying Catholic schools of Presentation Brothers College, my alma mater, and their bitter rivals Christian Brothers College.

For some reason, my father took me to soccer games on a Sunday but, even from a very early age, I made my own way to rugby games. I was eight years old and in first class, when I saw my first Munster Schools game and my beloved Pres were beaten by Crescent College from Limerick. I'm not sure when rugby moved to Musgrave Park but, in 1954, I queued for hours to get into the Mardyke to see the famous All Blacks. Munster were on level terms right to the final whistle and were only denied by a try in the corner, to lose 6–3.

Today, the ground looks exactly as it did on that day sixty years ago when 7,000 people crammed in. On visits to Cork, I periodically go through the gate and stroll around with eyes half-closed thinking of the sporting struggles I watched there.

2.   Lansdowne Road, Dublin

I am talking about the old ground here, not the soulless Aviva Stadium with its lunatic announcer, the appalling rock music, the awful Havelock Square End, the circuitous routes to get in and out of the ground, and the constant consumption of alcohol by the audience – to name but a few problems with that ground.

Lansdowne Road had character. Whether you had a few pre-match beers in a Baggot Street pub or frequented the more salubrious surroundings of Jury's and the Berkeley Court hotels, there was a wonderful pre-match atmosphere. The old ground was packed almost entirely by people from the clubs of Ireland and, standing on the terraces, you sometimes struggled to keep your footing as the heaving masses swayed with the excitement of the game. It was a place where you met old friends from Belfast, Cork, Limerick, Galway and emigrants at London Irish who made the trip to see the family and the rugby match, not necessarily in that order. The final whistle and the orderly move to the exits, shepherded by the dulcet, theatrical tones of Mick O'Dea in the announcer's booth. 'The level crossing gates are now closed. Please do not push towards the exits.' You knew all was well with the world.

3. Ballymore, Brisbane

I was asked by the coach of the American Eagles to be technical adviser for the first World Cup in Australia in 1987. I can remember very well where the invitation was issued – in the toilet of a bar in Berkeley, California. Ron Mayes was the coach of the Eagles and as we stood there, side-by-side, he turned to me and said, 'I would like you to help us in Australia.' I was shocked because, at that stage, I had never coached a representative team and here I was, about to be thrown in to the biggest rugby competition in the world. There was another first for me that night, as Mayes bought me my first ever sambuca – a simple guy from Cork had never seen a drink alight with a coffee bean in it!

The great adventure began on my forty-sixth birthday, when I left for Brisbane via Bangkok, without doing Ingrid the courtesy of telling her where I was going. England and hosts Australia were in our group, which made victories in those games unlikely. The opening game against Japan was in Ballymore and would determine the success or failure of the tournament for the neophyte Americans, almost all of whom had given up their jobs to take part. Rugby, then as now, wasn't a big deal in America. However, there was a bonus for these young men – on arrival in Australia, the expenses of the group were met by the Rugby World Cup organising committee, so for the first time, American rugby players got a *per diem* allowance. The game against Japan was won 21–18, and I can still remember the tense last few minutes as the Eagles hung on for victory. It was my first rugby international as a coach and I felt pretty chuffed. Back home, RTÉ was taking coverage of the games and the camera kept panning to me in the stands. It did a lot for my credibility in Irish rugby circles and Ingrid discovered, via television, where her errant husband had got to.

In 1987, Ballymore was the home of Queensland rugby and had a capacity of just 18,000. When we watched the matches, it was from the McLean Stand, which was named after the amazing McLean family who, between them, had played for Australia seventy-seven times. The outstanding member of the family was Paul McLean who was capped thirty-one times at fly-half, full-back and centre. In November 1981, he had been playing at out-half against Ireland and his cousin Peter was in the second row. In a bizarre coincidence, the match concluded with McLean kicking the ball into the Lower West End where it was caught by me – I still have it at home.

The great Paul McLean.

Pres V Christians

In Cork there are two fee-paying, boys-only Catholic schools: Presentation Brothers College, my alma mater, and Christian Brothers College. They are more familiarly known as Pres and Christians.

PBC is the elder by ten years, having been founded in 1878, and the two schools have helped form the bedrock of the professional and cultural life of the city. Students come from similar families and backgrounds, and the choice of school is very often because of past family history – or today by which school accepts the boy.

The big sporting tradition in both schools is rugby and because there are only two schools in Cork that play the game, the rivalry is intense. For many years this rivalry was such that they never met each other in friendly games. Only if they were drawn against each other in the senior or junior schools cup would there be a contest. Many boys went through their entire school career without ever meeting their closest rivals on the rugby field.

Happily that has changed and on the Saturday nearest to Christmas the two schools meet in the Mardyke to raise money for Share, the charity for the city's elderly citizens that was founded by Presentation Brother Jerome in 1970.

Today, the two schools also play rugby matches at every grade down to under-13. Previously, the only time Pres and Christians boys were locked in combat was in the contest for the girls at St Angela's, Scoil Mhuire, St Aloysius and the rest who engaged in the ancient Cork tradition of 'doing Pana', the after-school walk up and down Patrick Street where many romances began.

The early bragging rights for past pupils playing for Ireland and the Lions went to Christians. Mick Lane and Jim McCarthy went to New Zealand in 1950 and Noel Murphy, whose father had also played for Ireland, was a Lion in 1959 and 1966. A glorious era for Pres began when Tommy Kiernan was capped in 1960, to be followed a fortnight later by his classmate and good friend Jerry Walsh. Tom and Jerry both also played for the Lions.

The PBC half-back factory produced out-half Barry McGann and scrum-half Mick

Bradley but, most famously, Peter Stringer and Ronan O'Gara had been operating together since childhood.

With only Pres and Christians involved in rugby within the city, the thirty-odd players of the two schools cup teams in each year were courted assiduously by the clubs in Cork. Given that a large percentage played for UCC, the pickings were small but Cork, and in turn Munster, were rarely without a majority of players from the two schools.

The Munster Schools Cup at senior and junior level remains the big prize in any year. The senior cup established in 1909 has been won by both Pres and Christians on twenty-eight occasions – Rockwell is next with twenty-four wins. Because of the small number of rugby-playing schools in Munster, the competition has been dominated by the big three.

The same three schools tend to lift the junior cup too, and Pres leads the way with twenty-eight wins followed by Rockwell on twenty and Christians on fifteen.

I went to my first schools cup match in the Mardyke when I was eight years of age and in my first year at Pres. It was a senior cup match, and we lost to Crescent College. But it kindled in me, as it did in so many youngsters, the desire to wear the famous black and white shirt when I was old enough for cup rugby.

That was the day I heard for the first time the famous 'Tango'. It may not have the distinctive anthem feeling of Blackrock's 'Rock Boys Are We' but it would have a resonance for Zulu tribesman as they went to war.

Tango tango, walla walla whiskey
Yirrawaddy yirrawaddy, yup yup yup
Horam harum, hee hee hee
Napur naspur, qui qui qui
Yirrawaddy yirrawaddy, P B C

In the 1950s during my time at the school, Pres had the iconic figure of Pat Barry as coach, though in those days he was called trainer. Pat worked the night shift at the Dunlop factory in order to give him the free time to coach, so four times a week, he cycled to the school to coach the junior and senior teams. It was an enormous commitment.

Amazingly, there was no concept of friendly matches during that time, so the junior cup team would train all season and maybe have only one match if they were knocked out in the first round. On the other hand, the senior team did have a league before Christmas, called the Bowen Shield.

Pat Barry was tough, and he coached teams in his image. His aggressive style did not make him popular with other schools in Munster and, in 1958, Pres went on strike when the players were largely ignored by the Munster Schools selectors. Pat died suddenly in Musgrave Park at a relatively young age, having watched his beloved school team win the cup once more.

Sadly I never played for a junior or senior cup team for a variety of reasons, some of which stayed with me for most of my playing career but subsequently made me a much better rugby coach.

Pat Barry did not have time for individual coaching, nor in those more simple days was there an understanding of the mental side of the game. There were simply good players and bad players.

Despite being able to kick with both feet, pass respectably out of both hands and tall enough to provide a reasonable target in the lineout, I was massively lacking in self-confidence. I thought about the game too much and particularly what might happen in the tackle or the ruck. I persuaded myself that I was a coward. A more understanding coach might have made more of my talents and helped me with my weaknesses.

Rugby was everything in those days in Pres. I was an interprovincial cricketer, a discus thrower and a hand-baller, but that meant little in the pecking order of the school.

My lack of self-confidence halted my progress in club rugby, as it did in my career. I was, I suppose, the quintessential late developer. However, having to work out so much of the technical part of rugby for myself and ultimately conquering my lack of self-belief made me a good rugby coach.

I was good at teaching the skills of the game and above all imparting confidence to young men and women in whom I recognised some of my own failings. Today, right to the highest levels of rugby coaching, there is very often a lack of understanding of that crucial mental part of the game – something Joe Schmidt does seem to embody. On the other hand, Declan Kidney, whose entire career has been built on strong man-management skills, seemed to forget the ground rules in his dealings with Brian O'Driscoll and Ronan O'Gara at the close of their careers.

Today, things are very different in my alma mater and many types of sport are encouraged in tandem with high academic achievement. Principals like Brother Jerome and Mick Hennessy have left a strong legacy for their successors.

Memories are long and often unforgiving in schools rugby. If you talk to Tony O'Reilly, he never mentions his glorious moments for Ireland and the Lions but rather bemoans the lack of a Leinster Schools Senior Cup medal in his collection.

Declan Kidney is still reminded by some of his critics of his moment of madness in 1977 when playing against CBC in the Munster Senior Schools Cup final. He was the fly-half on the Pres team and inexplicably took a quick lineout to himself, was tackled and conceded the try that lost the cup for the school.

Years ago, I was speaking at the annual dinner of St Mary's College RFC. During the pre-dinner drinks, a couple of old Pres guys mentioned that Edmund Van Esbeck, then the rugby correspondent of *The Irish Times*, had lost a junior cup match for Pres by failing to catch a high ball under the posts.

I thought the story quite amusing and used it in my speech at the dinner. Sadly the recollection of my friends was faulty, and the distinguished journalist, who was in the audience, was not amused. Forty years on, the actions of schoolboys are still writ large on the reputation of adults.

The draw of schools rugby is strong – even more so in Cork where the internecine warfare between two great schools is acute. This year, I wore the tie of the Pres past-pupils union on television for a RaboDirect match. After the transmission, I received a text from Donal Lenihan, a former CBC boy, reading 'pity about the tie'.

Simon Zebo shows his early promise.

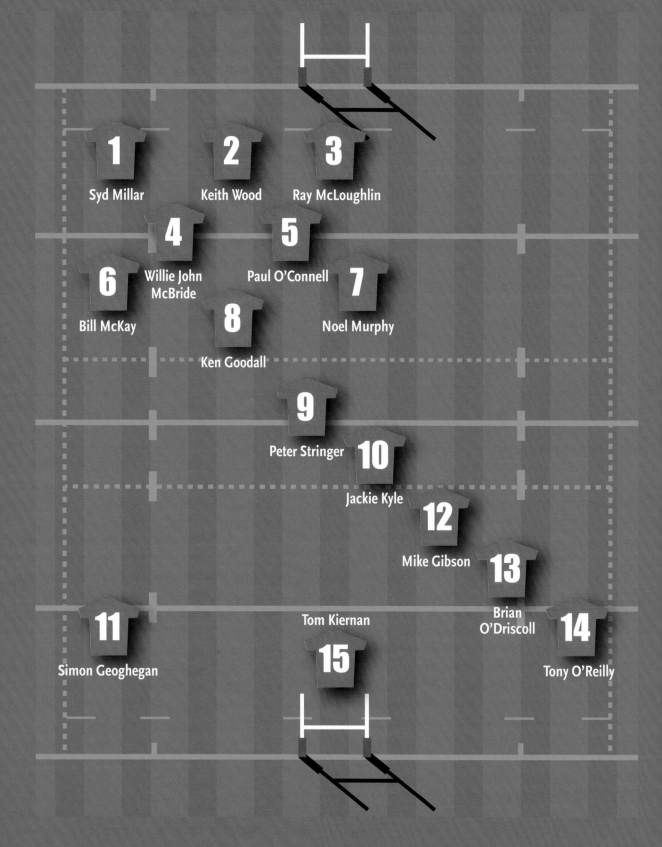

MY GREATEST IRISH TEAM

15 Tom Kiernan

Kiernan wins hands down over Jim Staples and Rob Kearney. The contenders were quicker, but Kiernan was the equal in every other area. He scores particularly highly for leadership, game appreciation and invention.

14 Tony O'Reilly

The greatest try-scoring wing in the history of the Lions was an automatic choice and requires no discussion.

13 Brian O'Driscoll

In the frame for the greatest rugby player of all time, O'Driscoll is a standout choice. No other three-quarter, let alone centre, has matched his physicality and raw courage. He has put his body on the line for every team he has represented.

12 Mike Gibson

The selection of the first four players was pretty easy and probably unlikely to cause much discussion. Gibson was without weakness and a professional with a small 'p'. His training regimes were legendary and as a former fly-half, his kicking game was superior to his partner in the centre.

Simon Geoghegan

The first awkward selection. Challenged by Brophy the defender, Crossan the finisher, Horgan of the magnificent physique and Hickie the try-scorer, it was never going to be an easy decision. Geoghegan makes the final cut on the basis of his wonderful athleticism, his amazing ability to beat defenders and perhaps not known importantly the fact that every team needs a joker.

Jackie Kyle

As Tina Turner would put it, 'Simply the best.'

Peter Stringer

Scrum-half, the position Barry John once said links the donkeys in the forwards with the intellectuals in the backs. It has always been thus. Given the position's crucial importance in linking the providers of possession with the strikers, passing has always been the first criterion for a scrum-half and, in this regard, Stringer had no peer.

Ken Goodall

In many ways, a postscript in Irish and Lions rugby. Yet, in what was almost a cameo career, Goodall displayed talents that made everybody who saw him wish that his decision to turn professional for Workington had simply never been made.

Noel Murphy

The problem for Murphy is that his open-side reputation rests purely on the early part of his career, whereas Fergus Slattery maintained the highest standards in the number seven shirt for his entire career. It really did boil down to a toss of a coin as they could not be separated even by the performances for the Lions.

6 Bill McKay

There may be a problem in selecting a player from over sixty years ago, but McKay's reputation for hardness exceeds Sean O'Brien, his try-scoring ability greater than David Wallace and his Lions tour of 1950 tipped the scales in his favour.

5 Paul O'Connell

He was first choice second row ahead of McBride! That says it all.

4 Willie John McBride

If only selection was always this easy!

3 Ray McLoughlin

Very little discussion here as the great technician took the prize, although he was run surprisingly close by Peter Clohessy.

2 Keith Wood

Each team of the different eras had at least two hookers in contention. At one point, it looked as if the selection might go with the hooker who did not even make the team of the quarter-century. However, Wood got the nod on the basis of a work rate that exceeded any of the competition. His individual skills also earned him top marks.

1 Syd Millar

Cian Healy lost out here because he is still a work in progress and Phil Orr because of doubts about his scrummaging. In the end, Millar's record was simply too good to ignore.

2015 RUGBY WORLD CUP

At the time of writing, the 2015 Rugby World Cup is just over two years away. Ireland has been drawn in Pool D alongside France, Italy, Americas 1 (most likely Canada) and Europe 2. Comparatively speaking, qualification to the knockout stage shouldn't be too difficult and new coach Joe Schmidt will target wins over France and Italy to top the pool.

But two years is a long time in rugby, and Ireland will arrive in England without Brian O'Driscoll, who has already signalled his intent to retire long before the next World Cup comes around. Doubts remain over whether Paul O'Connell, at thirty-three years of age, can continue for another two seasons, with a lot depending on how his body holds up in the intervening period, but the next twelve months will tell an awful lot.

The building process towards 2015 begins today. Schmidt will take over the reins with a squad very much in transition. The success of the Under-20 teams over the past three years proves that there is plenty of young talent coming through the system. It is an exciting time for Irish rugby and, with Schmidt as head coach, there is much to be positive about.

In this section, I look ahead to Ireland's opening match in 2015 and give my prediction on the starting team that might take to the pitch.

FRONT ROW
1. **Cian Healy**
2. **Richardt Strauss**
3. **Mike Ross**

Cian Healy will be a force to reckon with when the World Cup comes around. Prop-forwards take time to mature and develop but Healy has been growing into the loose-head role over the past three years. If he can hone his technique to match his raw physical power, it is frightening to think how good he could become. Mike Ross will be thirty-five in two years' time. It's not inconceivable that he will still be plying his trade with Leinster, given how late he came to professional rugby, but Ireland needs to develop more tight-head specialists. We've had a ridiculous situation over the past few years where John Afoa and B.J. Botha have occupied two of the four tight-head roles with the provinces. Until such time as another international-standard prop comes through, Ross will have to keep going. Schmidt needs to address this as a matter of urgency.

At just twenty-seven years of age, Richardt Strauss will be in pole position to start at hooker in 2015. His speed in the loose has been a huge asset to Leinster since he joined the province from the Cheetahs in the Super 15. Naturalised for Ireland in 2012, I expect the South African-born player to feature regularly for Ireland over the next few years.

Rory Best is approaching the twilight of his professional career and while he has been a loyal servant for Ulster and Ireland over the years, I wonder how much longer he can continue. His performances during the 2013 Lions tour have raised serious concerns over his management at lineout, particularly in pressure situations.

Mike Sherry is progressing really well at Munster, his leadership skills recognised by Rob Penney on several occasions last season, while Ulsterman and former Ireland Under-20 captain Niall Annett will also be pushing hard for a test place. Annett in particular is a tough, hard man who relishes the physicality of the front row. He is one to keep an eye on and could well challenge Strauss for the Ireland jersey in years to come.

LOCKS

4. Iain Henderson

5. Donnacha Ryan

Henderson is one of Ireland's brightest prospects and I believe he is the perfect fit for an international lock. Still only twenty-one years of age, he stands at six foot six and weighs over eighteen stone. The next two years will see him grow bigger and stronger. Ulster coach Mark Anscombe played Henderson in the back row for the majority of his first season in the senior ranks, but it would be a huge mistake to overlook his potential at lock. Ireland is blessed with an abundance of talented back-row forwards but with O'Connell not far off retirement, Henderson is my answer to our shortage at second row. I watched him play lock for the Under-20s and was very impressed by his mobility and skill in the lineout. Watch this space.

Donnacha Ryan, while not the biggest lock in world rugby, is the ultimate aggressor. His work rate is phenomenal and there are very few who can match his passion and commitment on the pitch. Ryan will be thirty-two at the next World Cup and his experience will be crucial in guiding Ireland through the tournament.

BACK ROW

6. **Peter O'Mahony**
7. **Sean O'Brien**
8. **Jamie Heaslip**

We have to assume that Stephen Ferris' playing days are almost at an end. At the time of writing, Ferris is twenty-seven years old and has just signed a short-term contract with Ulster until the end of 2013. Injuries have plagued him over the past five years and it is one of the great tragedies of Irish rugby that Ferris never really fulfilled his potential. All things being equal, I believe Stephen Ferris could have been one of the greatest players we have produced but fate dealt him a cruel hand. His knee has been damaged almost beyond repair. I hope there is light at the end of the tunnel for him but all the medical reports suggest his playing days are numbered. With that in mind, who else can fill the back row?

Peter O'Mahony has emerged as a real talent over the past two years. It wasn't long ago that he was lining out for Cork Con in the AIL. Now, he is a regular in both the Munster and Ireland camps. O'Mahony has that mad-dog Irishman attitude that cannot be coached or taught. Either you have it or you don't. His aggression is one of his main assets but I would like to see him add another stone of muscle to his frame. At twenty-three years of age, he has time on his side, but I would relish the chance to see an eighteen-stone O'Mahony running at opponents. He has all the ingredients to turn himself into a human wrecking ball. Hopefully he will live up to his potential. Sean O'Brien is another whom I worry about from an injury perspective. His physicality on the pitch is incredible to watch but it also leaves him vulnerable to picking up knocks.

Dominic Ryan and Jordi Murphy are both coming through the ranks at Leinster and I expect both to challenge hard for international places over the next two years.

Jamie Heaslip continues to sacrifice himself for the good of his team, both with Ireland and Leinster, and so much of the donkey work required to win the battles up front comes from the former Newbridge number eight. I expect him to hold on to his position in 2015.

HALF-BACKS

9. **Conor Murray**
10. **Jonathan Sexton**

Conor Murray's rise through the ranks over the past two years has been nothing short of incredible. Two years ago Murray was a twenty-one-year-old playing second fiddle at Munster. Today, he is a Lions scrum-half with international experience under his belt.

I thought long and hard about the scrum-half position because Murray will face an

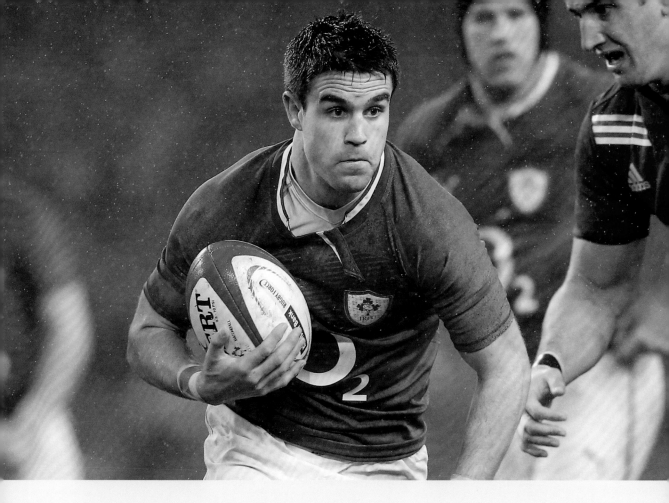

almighty battle for his test place from Luke McGrath over the next two years. The Ireland Under-20 captain has every ingredient necessary to make it at the top level and I expect him to be the starting Leinster number nine within twelve months. McGrath is lightning quick with a keen eye for a gap. His five-foot-nine frame masks an aggressive, tough player who is as good defensively as he is going forward. His tackling technique is straight out of a textbook. McGrath will push Murray all the way over the next few years and I wouldn't be at all surprised to see him start in the World Cup in two years' time.

The loss of Jonny Sexton at Leinster is huge. I certainly don't blame him for following the money to Racing Metro but it's unfortunate that we won't get to see as much of him in the coming years. Sexton's departure opens the door for Ian Madigan to shine. Again, Madigan is a player who has come on leaps and bounds over the past eighteen months. Leinster need look no further in filling the void at fly-half. Madigan is a ready-made replacement and his versatility in covering a number of positions means he must be considered as part of any international setup over the coming years.

CENTRES

12. Stuart Olding

13. Luke Marshall

Maybe a bit harsh on Fergus McFadden and Darren Cave who have been waiting patiently in the wings to take over from Brian O'Driscoll, but there are two young men in the Ulster camp who could dominate the Ireland midfield for the foreseeable future. I first saw Luke Marshall as a seventeen-year-old kid at the opening game for the Aviva Stadium when he was part of the Leinster/Ulster selection that took on a Munster/Connacht fifteen, and he simply blew his opposition backline off the pitch. Every time he got his hands on the ball that afternoon, he made ground. Eighty minutes and three tries later, the blond assassin had left his footprint on Irish rugby. Marshall, like Gordon D'Arcy, is blessed with a low centre of gravity which enables him to move quickly off either foot in limited space.

Stuart Olding has probably been fast-tracked on to the Ulster team a little quicker than even he would have imagined. The tragic death of Nevin Spence left a void in the Ulster midfield and Olding showed maturity and professionalism beyond his years to fill the inside-centre role. He is equally comfortable at fly-half and full-back but the Ulster coaching staff have marked him out as a centre. Olding is very quick and has an extremely effective boot. In two years' time, he and Marshall could be very dangerous in the Ulster and Ireland midfield.

WINGS

11. Simon Zebo

14. Craig Gilroy

Tommy Bowe will be nearly thirty-two by the time the World Cup comes around and while I expect him to be part of the Ireland squad, I'm not sure he will be first-choice wing by that stage. Simon Zebo has all the attributes necessary to be a superstar. The Munster man is quick, strong and talented and with his personality, good looks and happy-go-lucky attitude off the pitch, it's easy to see why he is universally liked. Zebo is a born finisher and if he continues to work on his defence there is no reason why he can't be an Ireland regular.

Craig Gilroy needs a lot of coaching over the next two years but his speed and ability to beat his man marks him out as a real talent. His kicking game and decision-making need work, but he is still young enough to get rid of any bad habits. Shane Williams and Will Genia are proof that size isn't everything. Gilroy's pace and footwork have the ability to make even the most seasoned defenders look foolish.

15. Rob Kearney

Rob Kearney is another player who has had more than his fair share of injuries. Because of this, he hasn't suffered the same attrition as other players of similar age. Kearney remains one of the most dependable men in the world under a high ball. His aerial ability wouldn't be out of place on a basketball court and his ability to read the game stands him apart.

Robbie Henshaw will probably have to leave Connacht to prove himself consistently at the highest level but the initial signs are very promising. It will be very interesting to see how Andrew Conway progresses at Munster and whether or not Rob Penney sees the former Leinster man as a potential full-back. If he does, with his pace and finishing ability, he might just emerge as a serious contender to Kearney's position.

OTHER INTERNATIONAL CONTENDERS

If Ian Madigan concentrates solely on fly-half at Leinster, he might miss out on an opportunity to develop himself as a twelve or fifteen. It all depends how Jimmy Gopperth fits in under new Leinster coach Matt O'Connor, but Madigan might be best served by keeping his options open.

With Ronan O'Gara gone from the Munster setup, J.J. Hanrahan has a real opportunity to make a name for himself. Questions remain over whether or not Ian Keatley is up to the task at fly-half, but I've seen enough of Hanrahan at underage level to be suitably impressed. He is a confident, strong young man with a big future if he continues to progress. It's a pity O'Gara hasn't stayed with Munster in a coaching capacity but, for me, Hanrahan is the future and should be the first choice fly-half from here on in.

Tom Daly is a big powerful centre in the Leinster academy. He was a regular in the Lansdowne team that won the 2012–2013 AIL title under Mike Ruddock and featured prominently for Ireland in the 2013 Under-20 Six Nations campaign. His goal kicking needs a bit of work but he has bags of potential. Daly's Lansdowne team-mate Mark Roche is also a very talented centre, blessed with pace and wonderful hands. I expect big things from both men in the coming years.

The future of the game

Where do we go from here? At the time of writing Ireland has suffered its worst Six Nations campaign in history. Declan Kidney's contract with the IRFU has been terminated and Leinster's Joe Schmidt has been promoted to the biggest job in Irish rugby. The future is uncertain in spite of the undoubted qualities of the new coach. Some of Ireland's greatest players are nearing the end of their careers and there are serious question marks hanging over those being prepared to replace them. The stagnant Irish economy continues to limit the amount of revenue potential for the game and with France and England attracting more and more foreign players, there is an increasing danger that Irish rugby will lose the battle to keep its best assets at home. No one can say with any degree of certainty what the future will hold. And that, perhaps, is most worrying of all.

I look back on the past fifteen years of Irish international rugby with an overwhelming sense of frustration. The optimists among you will point to a Grand Slam, four Triple Crowns and a number of scalps against southern-hemisphere opposition as cause for celebration, but I still feel Ireland has underachieved.

The Grand Slam in 2009 came four years too late. Looking back now, there is no doubt that Ireland had the players and the resources to dominate international rugby in Europe for nigh on ten years, but we managed only one Six Nations title during that time. While Munster and Leinster were destroying all around them in the Heineken Cup, Ireland were unable to put together five consecutive performances to win a championship title. We settled for Triple Crowns or the odd win against France and we pointed to the future trophies that would almost certainly come our way – but never did.

Now, as the final traces of our most gifted group of players prepare to fade into retirement, we look to the future and we are uncertain about what we see. Has Ireland blown its best opportunity in international rugby?

To find out where we might go from here, we must understand where we have come from. When rugby union went professional in Ireland at the end of the 1990s, the IRFU put in place a number of measures that were designed to give the national side and the four provinces every chance of competing with the top teams in the world.

Initially, it worked brilliantly. The decision to limit Ireland to four professional club sides enabled the IRFU to concentrate their resources on developing the cream of Irish rugby talent. Centralised contracts were awarded to Ireland squad players and added tax incentives for players to finish their professional careers at home dissuaded many of them from pursuing big-money moves abroad.

On the face of it, life was beautiful. Munster's heroic journeys in Europe captured the hearts of the nation and when they finally reached the holy grail by lifting the Heineken Cup in 2006, the entire country went rugby mad. This was a Munster team full of Irish rugby players. Only three of the twenty-six-man squad in the Millennium Stadium for the final against Biarritz that afternoon were non-Irish-qualified. Munster had set the standard and Leinster were not far behind. Between the two teams, Irish rugby fans would go on to celebrate an incredible five Heineken Cup triumphs over the next seven years.

The glory spread like wildfire. Young boys and girls flocked to see their rugby heroes whenever they could as rugby's popularity exploded. GAA strongholds complained of losing young talent to the oval ball, but there was very little they could do to stem the tide. Leinster and Munster regularly boasted 20,000 fans at mediocre league games as kids and adults everywhere began to take up the sport. It seemed the IRFU could do no wrong as the money flowed in from all angles and the goodwill generated from the success of the provinces fed through to the national side.

Except that the national side did not deliver. That breakthrough 2006 victory for Munster over Biarritz in Cardiff was supposed to be the catalyst for the national side to kick on and bring international rugby to the next level. But it never really happened. In the 2007 Six Nations Championship, Ireland failed to beat a very average France team in the first rugby international at Croke Park. Seven months later, in Paris, Eddie O'Sullivan's squad limped out of the Rugby World Cup in embarrassment when they failed to get beyond the pool stage of the tournament. Our golden generation of players had failed to surpass even the meekest of expectations, and nobody seemed to understand why.

In the thirteen years since the Six Nations was introduced, Ireland has won four Triple Crowns and just one championship title. To put that into context, France managed to win the Six Nations on five separate occasions, England on four and Wales also won four titles outright, including three Grand Slams. Further Ireland disasters along the way, including a hugely disappointing quarter-final defeat to Wales at the 2011 World Cup in New Zealand, left Ireland's international standing on a shaky platform of mediocrity. Worse still, large cracks in the IRFU system were beginning to break through to the surface.

The success of Munster and Leinster in European competition masked serious underlying problems within the Irish game. These shortcomings started at schools level, progressed through to the club game and materialised hideously in the professional ranks. And before anyone realised what was happening, it was already too late.

The severe shortage of international props best epitomises the IRFU's blinkered approach to the national squad. In a twisted take on Ireland's plight, if John Hayes had been half the man he was during his playing career, Ireland might have addressed the front row problems a lot sooner. But the Bull Hayes was a giant of a man and his relentless drive and determination to line out for his country kept Ireland's tight-head crisis at bay. And it was, indeed, a crisis.

Everyone could see what was happening, except for the IRFU. Fans, journalists and former internationals regularly pointed out Ireland's Doomsday scenario on the pitch, but nobody at rugby headquarters took any notice.

'What happens if the Bull gets injured? What happens if the Bull can't play? We'd be rightly f***ed, lads, there'd be no two ways about it!'

But the Bull kept on playing. Time after time, match after match, the man from Bruff put his body and his neck on the line for Ireland. And each time, he took his punishment, dished out some of his own, and kept on going and going and going. At the time, we watched with our hands in front of our faces. 'Keep at it, Bull,' we screamed, hoping to God that nothing bad would happen to our human pillar.

In hindsight, though, the best thing that could have happened for Irish rugby was the Bull refusing to continue. For we had absolutely no back-up plan whatsoever. There was no one else waiting in the wings, ready to come in and carry on the battle. We had all of our eggs in one giant basket and if that basket ever fell …

When Hayes eventually called time on his incredible career, Ireland turned to another man to carry on the tight-head burden. Mike Ross had just one provincial cap under his belt when he was deemed surplus to requirements at Munster. Like many Irish players before him,

Ross decided to pack his bags and head for England to try his luck. Harlequins head coach Dean Richards offered the twenty-six-year-old a three-week trial at Twickenham Stoop, but it wasn't long before Ross became a regular fixture for the Premiership outfit. Richards recalls watching his new player go up against an England international returning from injury in the summer of 2006 and 'more than holding his own'. Weeks later, on a pre-season tour to France, Ross packed down and scrummaged against a grizzled fixture in the French top flight and 'turned him inside out'. Richards couldn't believe his luck.

Ross went on to make sixty-two appearances for Harlequins during three successful seasons at the Stoop. He worked diligently on his technique under the close guidance of Richards and the pair developed a close working relationship. Richards picked up the phone 'countless times' to ask someone from the Irish coaching setup to come and have a look at his man for the national squad. Not a single phone call was ever returned.

When Ross left Harlequins after three seasons in London, he came back to Ireland to sign for Leinster in the hope of boosting his international chances. The timing worked out perfectly. Just as Hayes was nearing the end of his career, Ross was primed and ready to take on the mantle at tight-head. The IRFU had somehow struck it lucky for a second time and the gaping hole in Irish rugby was once again papered over.

Ironically, it would be two full years after Mike Ross had signed for Leinster – and gained his first cap against Canada – that he would make his Six Nations debut. Declan Kidney overlooked him time after time despite consistent performances by the Leinster player in the league and Heineken Cup. Only when every last rugby fan had screamed his name from the rooftop did Ross get a chance with the senior international team. His Six Nations bow came on 5 February 2011, against Italy in Rome.

Ross' career story thus far is a damning indictment of the protectors of the Irish game. A player with such obvious talent in an area where Ireland were desperately short should have been picked up and coached through the domestic system years before he ever left for England. That it took six years to bring Ross through to the senior team when even the most half-hearted rugby fan could attest to his talent speaks volumes about the lack of proper structures in place.

The system needs to change. The IRFU deserve enormous credit for putting the foundations in place that allowed professional rugby in Ireland to thrive in the early stages, but it has done too little to adapt to the changing demands of the game since then – and rugby is changing all the time. If the international squad is to maximise its potential, there needs to be a complete overhaul of how the game is run.

It starts when players leave school. The academy systems operating in the provinces are not maximising the potential of the players there. The current system is designed to spot the biggest and best players in their mid-teens, while they are still in school, and slowly incorporate them into a provincial setup.

If a player shows enough talent at fifteen or sixteen years of age, he is invited to participate in training camps under the guidance of the provincial academy. From there, depending on his progress, he will be offered an academy contract once he leaves school, but by this time the coaches involved will have a pretty good idea of what they can expect.

Life in the academy consists of approximately twelve training sessions per week. Academy players also develop life-management skills and are expected to commit fully to the provincial setup. Some are promoted to train with the senior squad from time to time, depending on their development. Players are also expected to keep links with their clubs and play for them as regularly as possible. After three years in the academy, those deemed good enough will be promoted to development contracts. Some sign development contracts after two years, but generally, the academy cycle is three years. Players on development contracts are still eligible to line out for their respective clubs but the problems start arising when a senior contract is signed. The current system of AIL clubs only being allowed to field two senior contracted players at any one time is ridiculous. It deprives clubs of their best players and, more importantly, limits the number of games for up-and-coming players.

The international prop shortage over the past few years best highlights the deficiencies and flaws in the academy system. Props, as a general rule, do not mature until their mid-twenties. How can a system that is specifically designed to pick out talented teenagers cater for guys who might not come into their own until they hit twenty-five or twenty-six? Cian Healy is certainly not a good example to hold up because he is the exception to the rule. Most men do not hit their peak physical strength until their mid-twenties, so how can a future international prop-forward be picked out while he is playing senior cup rugby in school?

Players are getting bigger every year. Precious skills that used to light up stadia across the world are slowly but surely being eradicated from rugby union. Size and bulk dominate the professional game and there is little sign of this trend reversing any time soon. If big continues to mean best, rugby union will become a game of bashing with little or no skill. Is that what we want to watch?

Some of the greatest moments in the game's history have come from the sleight of hand or the speed of foot from the smallest legs. Rugby has always been a game for all shapes and sizes. This simply must continue. One idea that I believe would improve the game as a spectacle has already been mentioned on a few occasions. Why not put the offside line at rucks and mauls ten metres back? It makes perfect sense when I think about it. Defences would be forced to rethink their strategy to cope with the additional space for attackers and the side with the ball would have more room to run. Giving the side in possession more space would lead to more tries and it would place the emphasis on speed and handling rather than brute strength. Isn't that what rugby should be all about?

The provinces will face huge financial challenges in the coming years. As television revenue increases in England, France and Japan, the amount of money on offer to players from foreign clubs will also increase. It can't be long before the IRFU faces the prospect of having to let the cream of Irish talent leave the country, because it simply cannot compete with the wages being offered abroad. Jonathan Sexton is the most recent high-profile name to leave Ireland and it will not be long before others follow suit.

Does anyone blame Sexton for leaving? I believe him 100 per cent when he says that rugby in France is not his preferred choice, but what option did he have? In France, he can earn in two years what it would take him five years to earn in Ireland. Where is the decision? In an ideal world, Sexton would stay with Leinster and see out his professional career in Ireland, but professional sport doesn't work like that.

There is also a much bigger problem looming on the horizon.

The European club tournaments are in real danger of disintegrating. The longer the dispute between the ERC, Sky and BT Vision drags on, the more likely it will be that the Heineken Cup will cease to exist in its current format. And that would be nothing short of disastrous for the Irish provinces. As I write, there are already strong whispers about the Welsh clubs abandoning the Celtic League to join forces with the Aviva Premiership in England. If that happens, the RaboDirect Pro12, as we now know it, could collapse altogether. A Celtic League without the Welsh clubs would be a huge step backwards and it would also greatly reduce the bargaining power of the remaining three countries to negotiate a new European tournament.

The Premier League in England is living testament to the power of television revenue. Without Sky shelling out billions of euro for live rights to Premier League games, English clubs would sink like stones in the sea. In order for the Irish provinces to sustain their current positions, they must be included as part of any negotiation for a European Cup. Without that revenue and exposure, the professional game here would die on its feet.

And then we have the Connacht problem. In the final Pro12 match of the 2013 season, a tired and drained-looking Connacht side were beaten by Glasgow Warriors in front of a packed house at the Sportsground. The game signalled the end of a number of careers in Galway, including head coach and long-serving Connacht legend Eric Elwood and the hugely popular open-side Johnny O'Connor. Hooker Adrian Flavin also retired that night after seven years of service and lock Mike McCarthy was leaving the west to join Leinster in the summer. It was an emotionally charged night in Galway but the performance of the home side did not live up to the occasion. Watching from the sidelines that night, I couldn't help but feel enormous sympathy for everyone involved.

In 2010, Connacht had an exciting, young squad that was preparing to compete in its first Heineken Cup campaign. But before it could do so, it was ruthlessly stripped of its star names. Wing and top try scorer Fionn Carr, hooker Sean Cronin and prop Jamie Hagan were all signed up by Leinster, while fly-half Ian Keatley departed Galway on a contract with the Munster squad. The spine of the Connacht team had been destroyed in an instant and the province was expected to soldier on through Europe's top competition without four key players. It all seemed grossly unfair.

Fast forward three years and none of those four men are excelling with their new clubs. Carr, Hagan and Cronin have all been reduced to bit-part substitute rolls at Leinster, while Keatley has so far failed to oust Ronan O'Gara from the number ten jersey at Munster. Imagine if those four players had stayed in Galway and committed their futures to Connacht? How much better might Connacht Rugby have fared with their services in the PRO12 and the Heineken Cup? The whole situation was farcical in the extreme and the IRFU just allowed it all to happen.

The success that Irish rugby has enjoyed over the past twenty years seemed to rise and fall with the Celtic Tiger. I'm not suggesting that the future of the game and the success of the Irish economy are somehow interlinked, but I do feel there is a strong correlation between the two. We may never experience the type of fiscal growth here that dominated the late nineties and turn of the century just as we may never again see Irish rugby compete so successfully in the Heineken Cup. Both situations are recoverable but both require significant and prudent investment.

If Ireland is to compete with the top sides in the world, it needs a structure from the top that will support and sustain any shortcomings or failings in the system. We need people in charge who know what the professional game is about and who understand what's required to make Ireland a successful rugby country. We either commit wholeheartedly to the professional game, from the schools and clubs, to the provinces and the elite national squads, or we continue our half-assed approach with mediocre results.

Rugby came to Ireland as an amateur game. It has evolved into a full-time professional industry. We embrace it or we get left behind. The latter is unthinkable.

'If big continues
to mean best,
rugby union will
become a game of bashing
with little or no skill.'

George Hook

Acknowledgements

This book is all my own work, apart from the contributions from Hugh Cahill which are clearly indicated. However, his involvement was much greater, in that he was an integral part of the early discussions, and his enthusiasm for the project, his willingness to help and, above all, his knowledge of the game were a vital component. Every writer has bad days and Hugh was always a willing shoulder to lean on.

Writing a book is a bit like the birth of an elephant – 'terribly simple in conception, but horribly difficult in delivery'. This book owes everything to editor Claire Rourke, who turned my prose into the final product you see today. Claire's knowledge of and regard for rugby was vital as she checked copy, sourced photographs and put a brake on my excesses. It took numerous breakfast discussions in McCabe's of Foxrock Village to finish the job and never were soft-poached eggs better or harder earned.

Ciara Doorley and Breda Purdue of Hachette Books Ireland took a risk in agreeing to publish a book based on little more than an idea on the back of an envelope. They never wavered in their support and I hope the finished article does justice to their faith in me.

Karen Carty of Anú Design has shown great imagination in her design of the book and, even to colour-blind people like me, has delivered a wonderful framework for the text.

Brian Byrne is a journalism student at DCU and a recipient of the Veronica Guerin Scholarship. He devised the graphic for the Grand Slam comparisons in a short timeframe and showed all the journalistic qualities required to meet a deadline. He will go far.

Willo Murray and I played together at St Mary's College RFC, but he is now without peer as a historian of Irish rugby. He was responsible for the statistics on the 1948 Grand Slam team which were vital to the comparison with the 2009 group of players.

Thanks also to Jack Cox for his research of names, dates, scores and venues.

This book gives me a belated opportunity to recognise the friendship and generosity of Ron Mayes who, in the decade between 1986 and 1996 as US Eagles coach and Chairman of the National Technical Panel at USA Rugby, gave me an opportunity to test my coaching skills. Without him my life might have taken a very different turn.

Jeffrey Archer, the English novelist, will be surprised to find his name here but when I interviewed him at his home in London he talked of the seanachaí, the storyteller. It gave me the idea to write the fictional chapter about the greatest Irish and Kiwi teams playing in Dunedin. I hope the great man approves.

Finally, my thanks to all the players past and present who, over six decades, have thrilled and excited me with their artistry, courage and commitment. Without their efforts there would be no book to write.

Permission Acknowledgements

The author and publisher would like to thank the following for allowing the use of their copyrighted material in *This is Rugby*.

page 1: © John Kane • page 5: © Inpho/Dan Sheridan • page 6: © Inpho/Donall Farmer • page 11: © RTÉ Stills Library • page 19: © Inpho/Cathal Noonan • page 27: © Irish Photo Archive (www.irishphotoarchive.ie) • page 34: © Getty Images • page 36: © Inpho/Billy Stickland • page 39: © Bob Thomas/Getty Images • pages 42–43 © Inpho/Dan Sheridan • page 46: © Getty Images • page 51: © Inpho/Morgan Treacy • page 57: © Colorsport • page 58: © Inpho/Billy Stickland • page 61: © George Kelly Snr • page 62: © Inpho/Ryan Byrne • page 66: © Inpho/Cathal Noonan • page 69: © Inpho/Morgan Treacy • page 70: © Inpho/Billy Stickland • page 73: © Getty Images • page 80: © Inpho/Dan Sheridan • page 83: © John Kane • page 86: © Inpho/Dan Sheridan • page 89: © Getty Images • page 90: ©Inpho/Allsport • pages 92–93: © Inpho/James Crombie • page 95 (top): © Colorsport/Colin Elsey • page 95 (bottom): ©Inpho/Allsport • page 97: © Inpho/Dan Sheridan • page 100: © Inpho/Dan Sheridan • page 102: © Inpho/Allsport • page 105: © AP/Press Association Images • page 110: © Inpho/Patrick Bolger • page 113: © Inpho/Billy Stickland • page 115: © Inpho/Allsport • page 119: © Inpho/Billy Stickland • pages 120–121: Gallo Images/Sunday Times/Avusa • page 123: © Colorsport/Elsey • page 128: © Getty Images • page 135: © Colorsport/Elsey • page 137: © Inpho/Billy Stickland • page 138: © Inpho/Billy Stickland • page 141: © Inpho/Getty Images • page 145: © Empics • page 146: © Empics • pages 148–149: © Empics • page 151: © Inpho/Tom Honan • page 152: © Inpho/Dan Sheridan • pages 144–145: © Inpho/Billy Stickland • page 157: © Getty Images • page 159: © Inpho/Billy Stickland • page 161: © Inpho/Patrick Bolger • page 163: © Colorsport • page 167: © Inpho/James Crombie • page 169: © Getty Images • page 172: © Getty Images • page 177: © Inpho/Billy Stickland • page 178: © Inpho/Billy Stickland • page 181: © Inpho/James Crombie • page 183: © Inpho/Billy Stickland • page 184: © Inpho/Billy Stickland • page 187: © Inpho/Billy Stickland • page 188: © Inpho/Patrick Bolger • page 191: © Inpho/Billy Stickland • page 192: © Inpho/Morgan Treacy • page 200: © Inpho/Billy Stickland • page 202: © Inpho/Morgan Treacy • page 205: © Inpho/James Crombie • page 208: © Inpho/Andrew Paton • page 211: © Inpho/Dan Sheridan • page 213: © Inpho/Photosport/Dave Lintott • pages 214–215: © Inpho/Patrick Bolger • page 216: courtesy Irish Examiner • page 219: © www.sporting-heroes.net • page 221: Presentation Brothers College, Cork • pages 222–223: Presentation Brothers College, Cork • page 225: Presentation Brothers College, Cork • page 230: © Inpho/Getty Images • page 232: © Inpho/Dan Sheridan • page 235: © Inpho/Billy Stickland

The author and publisher have endeavoured to contact all copyright holders. If any images used in this book have been reproduced without permission, we would like to rectify this in future editions and encourage owners of copyright material used but not acknowledged to contact us.

Index